The Role of the Bible in Contemporary Christian Education

The Role
of the Bible
in Contemporary
Christian Education

Sara Little

JOHN KNOX PRESS
RICHMOND, VIRGINIA

Library of Congress Catalog Card Number: 61-7497

Second printing 1962

Preface

Throughout Christian history, conflicting assumptions regarding the nature and significance of the Bible have emerged from or been determinative influences in the development of Christian thought. This is as true in philosophy of Christian education as in theology. Certainly the complexity and fluidity of the situation with respect to Christian education in America since the second quarter of the twentieth century relates in many ways to the varying conceptions of the Bible and its role in the life of the church. But the role of the Bible in Christian education has undergone crucial changes in recent years and is now moving toward a point of at least relative stability.

The new vitality and depth of concern generally evident in Christian education today and the new philosophy of Christian education now emerging seem to be closely related to the resurgence of interest in the Bible, in its message, its authority, its relevance. The identification and delineation of theories regarding the role of the Bible in contemporary Christian education might therefore be expected to have at least two results: first, to offer insight into the nature of contemporary philosophy of Christian education, with its achievements as well as its unsettled issues; second, and more important, to open the way for further exploration and clarification as to what role the Bible *should* play in the educational ministry of the church.

In considering the role of the Bible in Christian education today, this study is directed toward finding areas of consensus and divergence in thought as theoretical patterns are identified, with the hope that some contribution may be made toward the two results just indicated. The time seems particularly propitious for further consideration of the role of the Bible during this period when older curriculum patterns are breaking up and when probing questions are being asked concerning the role of the teacher in the kind of interaction that takes place when the biblical message is appropriated existentially within the experience of members of the Christian community marked by the presence of the Holy Spirit. Because of the conviction that one of the best ways to encourage and to contribute to this further exploration would be through focusing attention on some of the constructive thought already available, this study moves primarily in the realm of comparison and analysis of existing points of view rather than of presentation of an original thesis. It stems from a conviction that the Bible is, indeed, God's Word to man, and from the desire that Christian education should become an increasingly effective channel for the communication of the gospel.

The approach is to move through a consideration of the historical and theological background necessary for an adequate understanding of current concepts to an analysis of the role of the Bible in terms of four key issues faced today, and then to summarize and look toward the future. In the consideration of both the doctrine of revelation in theology and the issues affecting the role of the Bible in Christian education today, specific representative individuals have been chosen. The term *representative* is important, because writers have been selected out of a much wider survey and have been interpreted here as spokesmen. This approach, as over against that of reporting on a survey, has provided the opportunity for a more intensive analysis of the interrelationship of various aspects of thought than would seem possible in a more generalized approach. It is assumed that the brief introduction to the understanding of revelation of certain major theologians will be a readily accessible resource for Christian educators. With reference to the choice of James D. Smart, Randolph Crump Miller, and Lewis J. Sherrill* for special study, it should be said that these three seemed to "emerge" out of the study so naturally that their choice did not call for logical justification. Other persons might have been chosen, because the increased

---

* Dr. Sherrill died in 1957. Through his writings and his students, he continues to be a major influence in Christian education.

vitality in Christian education is producing capable theorists, but these three were chosen as representative of the "central core" of Protestantism today. The scope of the study is limited to this area of Protestant thought.

Perhaps two warnings should be given. The intent to find areas of agreement concerning the role of the Bible in Christian education may have given rise inadvertently to the impression that there is more stability than actually exists. Any person who teaches and is constantly considering controversial issues with colleagues and students knows that the climate is not one of complacency, although the controversies may rest on a more stable base than formerly.

Then, too, emphasis on theological thought may seem to suggest that this is the *only* influence that has entered Christian education. This, of course, is not the case. The doctrine of revelation was deliberately isolated as the factor to be considered. One of the reasons for this, among other more important reasons considered in connection with the study itself, is that it seems increasingly clear today that theology occupies a somewhat normative role in relationship to educational work. The educator needs to learn to co-operate with the theologian, not to compete with him or be forced to duplicate his work. If belief in diversity of gifts within the church is to be taken seriously, then those persons concerned to communicate the gospel will learn to think of specialized functions in terms of the total task. Of course this does not mean that Christian educators will passively receive and transmit theological ideas. The writers considered here have certainly not done that. It does mean that Christian educators are not autonomous. And it means that provision needs to be made for frequent, purposeful interchange of thought among many disciplines. Perhaps a part of the particular function of Christian education is to see that this is done.

What is written here may be more helpful to the minister or professional Christian educator or seminary student than to other readers. It presupposes a degree of familiarity with writings and terms in Christian education, and a background of understanding will make the comparison and analysis more valuable. But whoever reads, it is hoped that further thinking will be stimulated. Devoted and disciplined work is needed. And if the "dialogue" in "Toward a Point of View" has a tentative note, it is only because the author herself is still engaged in the process of "painful thought," looking expectantly toward a working together within the church of persons concerned to help and not hinder God's speaking through the Bible.

This book is based on research for the Ph.D. degree at Yale University. The author is permanently indebted to all who helped make that research possible, especially to Professor Paul H. Vieth, who continued to give valuable help as the book was being developed. Gratitude is expressed also to other Yale professors, Randolph Crump Miller, Claude Welch, and H. Richard Niebuhr, for what they have contributed directly and indirectly. President Charles E. S. Kraemer of the Presbyterian School of Christian Education has read the manuscript and made helpful comments. And many other persons, friends, family, and students whose contributions cannot be enumerated, have offered support and help in ways both tangible and intangible.

Presbyterian School of Christian Education
Richmond, Virginia
June 1960

Contents

I A Changing Perspective for Christian Education

The Present Situation

The nature and significance of the Bible are always of concern to the church and to Christian education. This is not less true, but more so, in these days following the dissolving of the traditional doctrine of revelation, when theologians seem to have reached a rather remarkable consensus concerning the reformulated meaning of revelation, days when Christian education, no longer belonging to the field of education, seeks a new home within the church and a new partnership with those theologians and biblical scholars who also stand within the church as servants of the Word. And, important as is the need for a theoretical formulation of Christian education that stems from the biblical message, no less urgent is the quite practical matter of helping the "man in the pew," obviously seeking after authority in a complex, never-static world, find answers for his questions about the Bible.

What, for example, is the average lay member of the church to think when he is told that in the Bible "God speaks" to him, that there God "meets" him "personally," that in his life as a Christian he is participating in the ongoing "drama of redemption"? What is the source of these and other related terms which are heard with increasing frequency, and what is the process through which they seem to be replacing the ideas, on the one hand, that the Bible is a series of infallible propositions or verbally inspired truths, and, on the other, that it is a "resource" written by men who, in their search for reality, have discovered and recorded those insights from their experiences which would help men meet their "problems" in later times? How, in these days, is the church helping men to hear when God speaks, to understand, and to respond in act and in being?

These questions are basic concerns of the emerging new philosophy of Christian education and of this study. Relating to key theological issues and originating in the current theological renaissance, they are in part the questions which helped a self-critical modern "religious" education, arising in the United States in the early part of the twentieth century, to become "Christian" education, rooted within the Christian community and explainable only in terms of the Christian heritage. This latest trend, focus of attention for this study, gives promise of being distinctive enough to be termed a new movement in Christian education. It became clearly discernible in 1947, the date of the report of the committee appointed in 1944 by the International Council of Religious Education (now the Division of Christian Education of the National Council of Churches) to re-study the whole field of Christian education. The report, published as *The Church and Christian Education,* with Paul H. Vieth, chairman of the committee, as editor, is as near a representative and official statement as it would be possible to get. It was followed in 1948 by the appearance of the Presbyterian, U. S. A., Faith and Life curriculum, a radically new approach to the use of the Bible, and a practical expression of the new theological interest. The same concern with the Bible evidenced here has continued to be a factor in sharpening issues and in developing an awareness of theoretical implications for curriculum construction and practices which have occurred since that time.

This is neither to say that this trend has brought clear-cut answers to the questions which have been raised, nor that there is one easily described philosophy of Christian education. Indeed, there are areas of both consensus and divergence in the attempted answers; and the questions which helped call forth new elements in philosophy of Christian education have in turn been questioned by that very philosophy. What has been suggested, instead, is that if there is a philosophy of Christian education in process of formulation, it is to be understood at least partly in terms of the impact upon it of what amounts to a rediscovery of the biblical message, and further, that the promise it holds forth can be realized only as it endeavors to deal adequately with matters relating to the Bible and its use. It therefore seems appropriate to raise the question of the role of the Bible in contemporary Christian education, but because the philosophy distinctive enough to be termed new is nevertheless continuous with the old, it is necessary first of all to inquire into the earlier understanding of the Bible in Christian education and into factors influencing change.

The Bible in "Modern" Religious Education

Modern religious education, in the technical sense of the term, may be said to have begun with the organization of the Religious Education Association in 1903. There was in this "modern" movement a definite continuity with the whole teaching tradition of the Hebrew and Christian communities. On the other hand, there was such an alliance with developments in twentieth-century educational philosophy, particularly with progressive education, that the different orientation may be said to have constituted a "new" movement. It was imbued with liberal theological presuppositions, and although it did not subsume everything that was happening in the Sunday school and other agencies, religious education of this day was precursor of and in contrast to the Christian education of the contemporary period.

The one word most descriptive of the Bible for leading religious educators by the third decade of the twentieth century seems to be "resource," which is a clear indication of how it was to be used. To understand why this came to be, one must go behind the scene to an earlier historical period and isolate at least two factors out of a complex situation—the new formulations of Schleiermacher and the development of higher criticism.

Friedrich Schleiermacher (1768-1834), unable to accept the authority of either reason or revelation as traditionally understood, found that a person's direct apprehension of God, his immediate awareness of reality, made his own experience a self-validating authority. What happened was that, inevitably, the whole matter of the Bible was brought into sharp focus. Authority, instead of being found in the deliverances of God, to be read and obeyed by man, was in the inner experience of the believer, in his relationship to and faith in Christ. Creeds and the Bible became important because they witnessed to this kind of faith in other people. Their significance was therefore that of "human" documents. The Bible was to be studied as any other book would be, and interpreted as any other book. Such a view of the Bible was decidedly different from that of the preceding century. It was a part of the "theology of religious experience" which provided the theological atmosphere so congenial to the development of higher criticism.

Criticism and analysis of historical sources, especially from the time of the publication in 1878 of Julius Wellhausen's *Geschichte Israels,* eventuated in rather radical conclusions concerning the Bible, more so in Europe than in America. Darwinian evolution and the scientific method seemed applicable to Bible study. What resulted was a wiping out of the emphasis on unity of revelation in the Bible, and a new emphasis on the influence of the environment in the growth of Israel's faith, leading to Jesus of Nazareth in whom humanity reached its highest peak of development, and in whom the divine could be most fully known. The prevailing point of view in America is nowhere better expressed than in the writings of Harry Emerson Fosdick. In his *Modern Use of the Bible,* published in 1924, he defined clearly what was considered the "new approach to the Bible."

> The total consequence of all the work of the Higher Criticism is that at last we are able to see the Bible a good deal as a geologist sees the strata of the earth; we can tell when and in what order the deposits were laid down whose accumulated results constitute our Scriptures.[1]

The concepts of progressive revelation and of "abiding experiences in changing categories" also marked the point of view, and the Bible was seen as leading man into a more abundant life marked by loyalty to Jesus and his way of life. Fosdick's later book, *A Guide to Understanding the Bible,* written in 1938, expresses lucidly the most constructive results of the liberal period. His point of view is that of a theist who sees in the process of biblical development a dual movement, both a human achievement and a divine self-revelation. Although the Bible represents final gains in apprehensions of truth, it also inaugurates a continuing development with an endless road open to the future.

Terminology employed by religious educators is different from that of theologians as transition is made from abstractions to such matters as curriculum. Nevertheless, it is possible to understand better the view of the Bible in "modern" religious education through reference to the two influences just cited, recognizing that these are not the only ones that were operative.[2] A brief look at the thought of two pioneers in religious education, George Albert Coe and William Clayton Bower, will make this clear. Existence of influence from the theory of learning developed by John Dewey will be equally clear as reference is made to theories about the nature of curriculum and the role of the Bible.

One of the founders of the Religious Education Association, and for more than forty years a professor and prolific writer, Coe is considered by many to be the leading philosopher in the modern religious education period. Certainly he has influenced every phase of development in Christian education since he transferred his major interest to this field, against a background of significant contribution in psychology of religion.

Coe's point of view with respect to the Bible was bound up with his concept of Christian education and of the nature of curriculum. His best-known definition of Christian education, although he has others, is this: "Growth of the young toward and into mature and efficient devotion to the democracy of God, and happy self-realization therein."[3] Here can be seen his emphasis on *growth.* This, as with Dewey, is a continuing process, an end in itself.[4] The growth which takes place occurs through *experience,* primarily through social interaction among persons, and not as an accumulation of the "dogmatic-intellectualistic" assumptions of a finished religion. Indeed, man is co-creator with God of this divine-human democracy, a moral order in which men are bound together by good will and by their recognition of God's working in, through, and with them. Coe could ask, then, "Shall the primary purpose of Christian education be to hand on a religion, or to create a new world?"[5] His answer is obvious. Whatever can be helpful in meeting the problems of creating a new world or in building personality—for Coe's emphasis on the infinite worth of persons and on God as the "Great Valuer of Persons" grew steadily with the years—is of value, be it the Bible, art, literature, or otherwise.

Such a concept of Christian education would automatically do away with the older, more static concept of curriculum. "Content" would be social experience, not printed facts to be mastered. Faith would become meaningful, not through telling and commanding, but through " 'living epistles,' known and read in family, church, or Sunday school."[6] Curriculum construction for Coe rested on theological foundations and employed to the fullest the experience which educational psychologists saw as means for growth and theologians saw as the area of self-validating religious authority.

What does this mean for the use of the Bible? Coe's own words are quite clear at this point.

> The consequence for religious education is that it consists primarily in the awakening of religious experience in children through their contacts with persons who already have such experience. The Bible then takes its place as a means that mightily assists in promoting, illuminating, and confirming these contacts, and in extending the Christian fellowship backward to Jesus and the prophets, and forward toward the fulfilling of the prophetic ideals.[7]

For Coe, then, the Bible was a "means," to be used in "the interest of present living." It could be so used because it was a "transcript of life" and not a body of doctrine, an occasion for Christian experience and growth and not for indoctrination.

William C. Bower, one of Coe's students, is another early

leader. A teacher and writer, he was for many years an influential participant in the International Council of Religious Education's work on curriculum. His theory of curriculum, one of his chief contributions to educational thought, centers around his concepts of *knowledge* and *experience*.

Knowledge "arises out of experience as meaning," and then "re-enters it as a factor of control," where it is validated.[8] Truth therefore does not consist of fixed formulations so much as of hypotheses or tentative working conclusions to be used in experience. At no point can knowledge and experience be separated. Personality development itself depends upon the organic unity of these two, for personality is a "dynamic and organizing centre of a continuum of experience that is constantly undergoing reconstruction."[9] The nature of curriculum now becomes clear: it is to be thought of "in terms of enriched and controlled experience."[10] This phrase appeared so often it actually became almost a catchword for the period. Evidently Bower is the first to have used it. It does express concisely the undiluted concept of curriculum in which the Bible has value as it contributes to the ongoing experience of persons.

How would it be used in this way? Bower sees three elements in curriculum—the situation, the past experience of the learner, and the experience of others. It is at this third point that the Bible enters, because it is an account of the religious experience and growth of individuals and groups. Passages for use are to be selected on the basis of their correspondence with present experience, their inherent social, ethical, and spiritual values as applicable to the present. The supreme criterion is "the degree to which it approximates the mind of Jesus and furthers the progressive realization of the ideals of the Kingdom of God in the larger and more difficult human situations of our times."[11] Insofar as the Bible passage approximates the criterion, it has a "distinctively Christian quality" and is valuable in the curriculum. Moreover, the Bible again becomes "the Living Word" whenever it is functionally related to "the going experience of the continuing religious community out of whose earlier experience it had its rise."[12]

An abundance of material was available for this period to interpret to laymen the changing concepts of the Bible, its origins and development.[13] If people were uninformed about the results of historical criticism, it was not because of a lack of interpretive materials. Writers on teaching recognized newer developments, and interpreted their implications for methodology. Ethel Smither's *The Use of the Bible with Children* (1937) portrays the Bible as "the best guide and inspiration in the age-long quest for God and for the meaning and justification of life."[14] Attacking the problem of "the Bible and children," the book was so successful that it was in continuous use until the appearance in 1960 of Miss Smither's new book, *Children and the Bible*.

Method in Teaching Religion (1925), by George Herbert Betts and Marion O. Hawthorne, is a book written for advanced students, and served as a textbook for years. In it, the Bible is definitely to be used as a source book, and knowledge is valuable insofar as it will function as a guide to conscience and conduct. But there is still a recognition of the Bible as content and heritage, as a body of knowledge to be taught. Paul H. Vieth's book on teaching, *How to Teach in the Church School* (1935), shows the same tendency to go beyond the view of the Bible as resource. Although the Bible helps to achieve life's values and to re-create religious experiences within the present generation, it is "the Word of God . . . a record of the highest revelation of God to man." And "the one note which runs through the entire Bible is that God is concerned with human life and that man's business is to do the will of God."[15]

Even such glimpses as this indicate variations in emphasis, variations which existed in spite of the fact that many people assumed liberal theology to be normative for religious education during the early days of its development as a "modern" movement. Adelaide Case, in a 1924 study of objectives, made this assumption, and in her evaluative remarks reflected her concern that certain recognized leaders of religious education—Betts, for example—did not meet liberal standards in all respects. She called attention to the fact that the American Sunday School Union, formed in 1824 and one of the influential interdenominational movements, did not accept reconstruction of experience through use of the Bible as one of its objectives. For them, the Bible was primarily God's saving message for mankind.[16]

It was not only the American Sunday School Union that raised questions, however. To say that the theory of Coe and Bower concerning the role of the Bible was accepted universally would be to overlook the varying emphases among the numerous other writers who spoke on the subject—and probably at no other period in the history of American religious education have there been so many capable theorists in the field, men like Athearn, Cope, Ames, Soares, Weigle, and others. Walter Athearn had many questions concerning the thought of Coe and Bower.[17] Luther Allan Weigle, an influential force through his teaching and writing, as well as through his service in denominational and interdenominational agencies, consistently refused to see education and evangelism as opposed forces. He maintained a balanced perspective which took into account a "creative education" related to experience, but never in separation from the gospel or the God who reigns and acts and moves in history toward the accomplishment of his purpose.[18] Other illustrations could be given of the rich diversity of thought, but the more important thing here is to get a glimpse of the main stream of change as it leads up to the contemporary period.

The nearest to an official statement would be expected from the International Council of Religious Education, serving as a clearing house for Protestant education since its origin in 1922. Such a statement is to be found in the Council's officially approved *Objectives in Religious Education,* by Paul H. Vieth, accepted as basic for religious education since 1930. Based on the studies of the writings of ten recognized leaders in religious education and four in public school education, the statements of seven comprehensive objectives include one related to the Bible. That objective is stated as follows: "To effect in growing persons the assimilation of the best religious experience of the race, as effective guidance to present experience."[19] The statement relating specifically to the Bible reads thus: "To lead growing persons to a knowledge and an appreciation of the Bible," with a subdivision, "The Bible as a record of developing religious experience; its meaning for the life of today."[20] This statement of objective seems to substantiate what Erwin Shaver saw as a trend in 1928, the use of the Bible as a source book—a source for principles of living, for symbols and codes, and a dynamic source for ever-enlarging revelation.[21]

Conflict and Transition

Evidence of divergence within prevailing trends has already been suggested. Conflict came out into the open, and by the late 1930's religious education, which had earlier been hailed as the new pathway to salvation, came under violent attack. Signs of the attack may be seen in Georgia Harkness, who, writing in 1931, could confess to "a feeling of depression" on reading religious education books, and to an impression of "the absence of any clear idea of what the whole thing is driving at."[22] Her basic contention, to be heard frequently from others in the next few years, was that religious education emphasized too much the "how" and too little the "what" of education. There were other criticisms, too, but the question of the content of education made the role of the Bible one of the central issues. Influences from Barth's writings would have directed attention to the Bible even had there been no other impetus, just as Reinhold Niebuhr's questions about man and society threw a bombshell into complacent assumptions about the dignity of man or his "happy self-realization" in the "democracy of God." E. G. Homrighausen came early under the influence of Barth. The real problem, he said, was that religious educators, in accepting Dewey's underlying assumptions, had placed man himself as authority, whereas the situation is that religion "must not start with autonomous man, but *with divine thought about man*."[23]

The conflict is focused most sharply in Harrison Elliott's *Can Religious Education Be Christian?* (1940) and H. Shelton Smith's *Faith and Nurture* (1941). Elliott, adhering closely to the progressive religious education approach, objected vigorously to anything approaching a teaching of the Bible by "instruction and indoctrination" and saw many dangers in the increasing neo-orthodox influence. He stated his conviction that thorough historical study of the biblical records, carried on without preconceived ideas of what one should find, is basic to an understanding of the meaning of the Christian faith. Moreover, this kind of approach is essential if biblical records are to be used effectively in helping people face their own problems. The purpose is not to *copy* experiences of others, but to find through correct insight into those experiences illuminating help for oneself and the world.

Neo-orthodox interpretation stands in direct contrast to this view, Elliott said. It recognizes the importance of historical study, but not because such study helps make the past intelligible and relevant to the present. Whereas for Elliott reason and experience are channels for revelation, for neo-orthodox interpreters the "meaning of that history in which God manifested himself in Christ is revealed only to faith."[24] What happens, Elliott said, is that "instead of coming to the Scriptures with open mind and heart, asking God to illuminate their understanding, they really come with convictions already formed and ask God to confirm those convictions through the Scriptures."[25]

But this is impossible for the Christian educator. For him, the educational process is an approach to life and not a methodology for transmitting preconceived ideas. God reveals himself in nature and history as well as in Jesus Christ, and the Scriptures are to be used to help interpret present events, to aid in the development of one's own experiences and beliefs, and to make possible the continuing development of the Christian religion. Such, in brief, is Elliott's position with respect to the nature and use of the Bible.

H. Shelton Smith was severely critical of such a view. To him it said that the Bible had been made into a stimulus for "a religious quest that will result in the creation of spiritual norms that transcend those embodied in the Bible."[26] As he saw it, the main concern of progressive religious education was not with "the recovery of any particular past religious insight, but with the process of remaking all insights,"[27] and the "technic of thought" was more important than the "content of thought." These are heresies to Smith. His own position will have to be assumed, gathered from that which he opposed, for his work is "critical reconsideration" as the beginning point for what he hoped would be "a way forward." Certainly he succeeds in pointing up issues sharply, but what this means for the practice of religious education is not touched upon, except by way of implication. The issues are theological.

As early as 1940 there was evidence of a changing mood in *Christian Education Today,* an International Council of Religious Education publication. It is a "Statement of Basic Philosophy," written by a committee under the chairmanship of Dean Luther Weigle. Although this committee does not deny the soundness and continued usefulness of basic insights from the preceding period, there is a strong note of emphasis on the linkage of the present with the Christian heritage, an unequivocal stand on the reality and power of God as the "source of all existence," and a concern that Christian education should be "animated by Christian faith" at the same time it helps "reinterpret Christian faith."[28] But there was not yet a readiness for major change, and polemical discussions continued.

Secular education, moving through attacks and changes which both paralleled and influenced those in religious education, did seem to find a "tenable middle ground" by 1945. At that time a rethinking of educational theory resulted in a Harvard publication which has since become a landmark.[29] *General Education in a Free Society* attempts to present a balanced view which, though "apt to be less immediately striking" than an extreme view, "aims to do justice to the whole truth in all its shadings."[30] Thus, whereas education in the immediate past had seemed to place more emphasis on the open mind and change than on heritage, the true task of education is to reconcile the "necessity for common belief" and a "sense of pattern and direction deriving from heritage" with "the equally obvious necessity for new and independent insights leading to change."[31] Indeed, "nature abhors an intellectual vacuum," and "a measure of belief is necessary in order to preserve the quality of the open mind."[32] Change comes from within commitment. Freedom does not exclude authority. "We believe that men are not in any genuine sense free to choose unless the fullest possible truth is presented to them. That is to say, freedom is not permission to flout the truth but to regulate your life in knowledge of it."[33]

There is certainly no decisive break here with pragmatism or scientific method or progressive education, but neither are they acceptable without severe modifications. The "balanced view" which results combines elements from the old and the new.

The same role which *General Education in a Free Society* plays in education in general, Paul H. Vieth's *The Church and Christian Education* fills in Christian education. Published in 1947, the book recognizes values in the old, but marks the transition to a new day. Christian education deals with "more than our human quest for the good life."[34] It has to do with that which is "divinely given," and with the affirmation of Christian faith that *"God has revealed himself within history."*[35] When the term "revelation" is used, it refers primarily to "the acts of redemption to which the Bible points," rather than to "noble insights."[36] Yet the special revelation in the Bible and in Jesus Christ does not exclude general revelation. It only points to the fact that Christian faith roots in the Bible, in "certain events which occurred in the first century and the interpretation put on those events by those who first experienced them."[37] Therefore, "Christian education cannot do less than present these facts and convictions with all the weight of authority" attributed to them by history and the church.[38] At the same time, this faith which roots in the Bible can become meaningful for a person only when it is *his* faith, appropriated through *his* experience.[39]

By 1947, then, the atmosphere in Christian education had changed to the point where it became necessary to reconsider the whole matter of the role of the Bible in Christian education. The problem is one which is crucial at the present time.

Revelation and the Bible

If it is true that the period of relative stability of thought during the modern religious education period was undergirded by clearly definable theological presuppositions, it is also true that the period of conflict and transition just considered was at least partially set in motion by the upheaval in theological thought. In fact, the moment of greatest seeming stability is often the very moment of death of an old era or birth of a new. Harry Emerson Fosdick's *A Guide to Understanding the Bible* was referred to as a significant liberal interpretation of the Bible. It has been cited by Bernhard Anderson, quoting Walther Eichrodt, as having summarized the prevailing view of Fosdick's generation, but also as having presented "the obituary of a whole scholarly approach and method of investigation, making both their inherent merits and their limitations clear to the thoughtful student."[40]

Any consideration of the *Guide* as an "obituary" must take into account the fact that it was written in 1938, when momentous changes were already under way in almost every phase of biblical and theological thought. Probably no change was more crucial than that developing in the doctrine of revelation. It is important to consider the nature of this change if the perspective in Christian education is to be understood, but first one ought to look directly at the question of why the doctrine of revelation is so important in the educator's understanding of the role of the Bible. Lewis J. Sherrill says the doctrine of revelation is "a crucial element in the life of the Christian community and in the philosophy of Christian education. Indeed, it could be maintained that it is the determinative element in both."[41] When revelation is equated with the words of the Bible, then the church can turn to the Bible as an objective authority, and the task of Christian education is to offer biblical instruction. When revelation centers in religious experience, then the Bible is a valuable human document to be used as a resource in teaching, and its authority is primarily subjective in nature.

It is this second approach which characterized the so-called modern religious education of the early twentieth century, and which was instrumental in the dissolution of the Thomistic view of revelation. Problems focused by this "traditional" Thomistic view and the conflict with it continue to be crucial today.

Throughout the greater part of Christian history, John Baillie says, any intelligent schoolboy could give an answer to the question of the meaning of revelation.[42] He would do it in terms of the distinction between revealed and natural knowledge, indicating the two ways by which men have gained knowledge of God. Perhaps this interpretation is most directly attributable to the thirteenth-century writings of St. Thomas Aquinas, whose theological formulation of the doctrine of revelation became normative both inside and for many outside Roman Catholicism. Natural knowledge of God, achieved by the use of man's own reason, was supplemented by revealed knowledge, a direct communication from God himself, which did not contradict but rather verified the first, in some ways duplicated it, and in many ways gave access to knowledge not attainable at all by the exercise of unaided reason. The equating of revelation with the communication of the body of supernatural knowledge in the Bible has been challenged more than once in the history of the church, and the dichotomy between reason and revelation has given rise to controversies which persist to the present day.

Observation about contemporary Protestantism, for example, might lead to the generalization that one strand of thought, accepting essentially the Thomistic synthesis on revelation, adheres to the supernatural biblical revelation as infallible; this line stands in a stream which has perpetuated an extreme emphasis on the Reformation principle of *sola Scriptura* through the days of Protestant scholasticism and its demise to the present fundamentalism. At the other pole is the strand of thought which, unable to accept the Bible as inerrant, propositional revelation, chooses the way of reason. This second strand embodies forces opposing acceptance of any knowledge as supernatural from the days of the Enlightenment through a later devotion to science to the present religious or scientific humanism, or such movements as Unitarianism.

But the central core of Protestantism today has not chosen one alternative as over against the other. Nor has it been able to accept the alternative offered in the liberal synthesis which effectively undermined the traditional doctrine of revelation. What has happened, instead, is that within that central core there has emerged a different understanding of revelation and therefore of the nature and significance of the Bible. Whether the "newer" will become normative has yet to be determined.

It is recognized, of course, that the theological view of revelation is not the only factor which influences the educator's understanding of the Bible's role in the communication of the gospel. Yet it is a key factor. Thus it is necessary to inquire somewhat precisely into the theological and scholarly understanding of revelation and of the Bible. This study proceeds in that direction. Even so, it is to be noted that fundamentalism and other theological modes of thought still parallel, penetrate, and limit what will shortly be considered as patterns of thought characteristic of the contemporary scene. That fact is to be constantly remembered, although attention here is to be directed primarily to that central stream of change continuing in motion through the operation of "the Protestant principle."

II The Theological Influence

Contemporary theology, beginning approximately in 1918 on the continent with the publication of Karl Barth's prophetic *Römerbrief* and in America in 1932 with Reinhold Niebuhr's *Moral Man and Immoral Society,* has an atmosphere quite different from that of the nineteenth century. There is a recapturing of many of the traditional modes of Protestant thinking, but modes of thought now reinterpreted. Emphasis is on the fact that God takes the initiative in disclosing himself; man responds. Now it is more a matter of Anselm's "faith in search of understanding" than of the Thomist's "faith completing understanding."

What brought about this kind of change? The disillusionment following World War I and the Depression resulted in what some have called a "failure of nerve." Human effort was distrusted; pessimism about man and his possibilities prevailed. The democratic ideal, to which America gave lip service, somehow did not eventuate in a real trust in democratic processes. Totalitarianism arose in several governments, education cried aloud for a return to the essentials, and theology, interacting with other areas of thought and with historical forces, moved to a new position. Some of the "assured results" of biblical criticism turned out to be not so assured. Efforts to find and portray the historical Jesus led to the recognition that he could not be separated from first-century Judaism, nor from the early Christian community, nor from tradition. Barth's affirmation that man needed God's Word *to* him, not his word *about* God, again raised the question of authority. The religious experience which liberalism had placed as the foundation of Christian knowledge was seen to be so culturally conditioned, so relative, that it was far less reliable or permanent than the Bible. Thus the pendulum moved, propelled by a configuration of factors too complex to be specified in detail.

One key factor, however, the concern with the doctrine of revelation, brings into focus the theological thought as it influences the role of the Bible in Christian education. Something of the scope and nature of the current understanding of revelation is to be considered as it is reflected in the distinctive and varying emphases of five representative major theologians whose influence is evident in educational circles of that portion of Protestantism participating in the National Council of Churches. Doubtless the time will come when another major theologian, Bultmann, will influence Christian education, but at present his impact is primarily on the field of theology. Other theologians are not considered, even though their influence is apparent, because their contributions seem to be included within the emphases covered here.

Revelation and Experience: William Temple

To speak of revelation as the "coincidence of event and appreciation," or to proceed from the assumption that in revelation one meets "the living God Himself" is to refer to concepts characteristic of the newer understanding of revelation given almost classic formulation by William Temple in his *Nature, Man and God*. As an Anglican theologian, he is representative of that temper and frame of mind in which Walter Horton sees the best opportunity for a new consensus to replace the older Thomistic and Protestant scholastic consensus disrupted during the past hundred years.[1] Temple's thought is to be considered as representing the continuing liberal tradition, not only with respect to general revelation, but also with reference to the emphasis on religious experience as the medium for revelation. This is a liberalism modified by the complex changes in theological climate during the twentieth century, as is indicated by the fact that his views hold even the possibilities of a synthesis. Temple was still writing up to the time of his death in 1944, and although he is no longer directly contributing to theological discussion, his position brings into focus views widely prevalent in that group of contemporary evangelical liberals concerned to conserve the best of the liberal tradition. Persons like Georgia Harkness, Harris Franklin Rall, Herbert Farmer, or others might be cited, but Temple has been chosen as the best spokesman for the group.

Five points of central importance to Temple's concept of revelation are to be considered.

Religious Experience

In a summarizing statement, Temple has this to say:

> The essential revelation is an act of God apprehended in a complete living experience, in which subjective and objective factors are both active; it is not capable of isolation from that experience, and is only renewed so far as the experience itself is recovered or renewed. Sacred writings and authoritative formulae are not themselves the substance or reality of revelation. That is always the living God Himself, and nothing less or other. But sacred writings and authoritative formulae may contain the record of the divine act which actually is the revelation, and point the way to recovery or renewal of the experience in which it is apprehended.[2]

This quotation points up clearly the importance attached by Temple to the "living experience" which is, in the Reformation tradition, a faith-response of the whole person to the God who makes himself known to man. It is through this emphasis that Temple conserves that vital contribution of liberal theology formulated most impressively by Schleiermacher. Probably doctrine is more important for Temple than for Schleiermacher, but it is not primary. What is primary for both men is a personal fellowship with the living God. Doctrines are interpretations of the revelation received through experience. But the kind of religious experience of which Temple speaks should never call forth the accusation of "psychologism." He refers to religious *experience* rather than *experiences,* to a constant apprehension of the divine ordering of the universe which becomes a quality of life pervading the whole experience of religious persons and a context for the special moments when they do occur. That specific form of religious experience to be termed revelation occurs when there is an apprehension and appreciation of the divine self-disclosure manifested in objective events.

Temple considers the subject of authority in relation to religious experience. He does it because, for him, the authority inherent in the self-disclosure of the divine character and intention becomes operative only for and within those who experience the response of surrender to this disclosure. Authority lies, therefore, not in personal experience itself, but in the nature of God as apprehended in religious experience.[3] There is an authority of tradition, and of the record of revelation, but the personal response of worship and obedience is ultimately the way by which spiritual authority is exercised over a man, for *"the essential principle of spiritual authority is the evocation by Good of appreciation of itself."*[4]

Event and Appreciation

What has been said about religious experience is related to Temple's understanding of revelation as *"the coincidence of event and appreciation."*[5] To describe revelation in this way is to say that it always consists of both subjective and objective aspects. In fact, that specific religious experience which is "apprehension and appreciation" is but the subjective aspect of revelation. This is not an accidental coincidence, but an essential condition of revelation; it is the coming together of "divinely guided events with minds divinely illuminated to apprehend those events."[6]

It should be noted that with Temple the objective takes priority over the subjective. This means that the *facts* of which the biblical writers were conscious—the events of the Exodus, for example—occurred before the awareness of those events. Thus, while the Bible affirms the unity of the record of the religious experience of Israel and of the revealing acts of God, the primary emphasis is on the latter. Analysis is not of the religious consciousness, but of the historical acts of God. Men are divinely led to see the *meaning* in objective events.

Thus God has chosen the way of guiding external events in which man is enabled to see his hand instead of the way of "introducing ideas." There is no "revealed truth," then, but there are *"truths of revelation."*[7] The Bible is not a repository for ideas but is a record of God's revealing acts and their meaning.

The Living God

In the revelation which is an "intercourse of mind and event" one enters into fellowship with God. This has been suggested several times, but it is so important that special attention needs to be called to it. Probably the majority of contemporary theologians would agree at this point.

The refusal to think of either God or person as "it," so strong in Martin Buber, is found also in Temple:

> *Every revelation of God is a demand, and the way to knowledge of God is by obedience. It is impossible to have knowledge of God as we have knowledge of things, because God is not a thing. We can only know a person by the direct communion of sympathetic intercourse; and God is personal.*[8]

Lest it should be concluded that this self-disclosure of a personality to persons means only an experience of awareness, reference should be made to Temple's concept of authority. The very nature of that which is revealed exerts an intrinsic authority upon those whose eyes are opened to see. In this case, it is the holy and righteous God who is revealed. Revelation, as the self-disclosure of God, is thus the basis for the ethical life of the Christian.

Jesus Christ the Supreme Revelation

If God is to disclose himself as Person to men as persons, he can do this most fully in the life of a person who is one in essence with himself. This does not mean that Jesus Christ is the *only* revelation or the full content of revelation. All earlier, provisional truth is caught up in and possessed by him, so that the whole reality of revelation comes to focal expression in Jesus. He is the culmination of revelation.

The central importance of the Incarnation does not lie in the fact that the divine Word clothed himself in general humanity. The fact that in "Christ the Truth" God appeared at a particular time and a particular place, living a life culminating in actual death and resurrection, is an occurrence "beyond all comparison the most important in history," because it is the event of "the taking of Manhood to the throne of God and the indwelling of God in the hearts of men."[9] And "all human history from that time onwards is the process of eliciting man's answer"[10] to the fullness of God's revelation in Jesus Christ.

The Sacramental Universe

A point of major emphasis in Temple's thought, one likely to provoke controversy, is his concern that general revelation be recognized both as the condition of man's "natural knowledge" of God and as an essential to any belief in special revelation. There is no discrediting of reason in Temple, and no hesitancy to employ philosophy where it is helpful. When a statement like this is made, it is important to note that Temple considers the old distinction between natural and revealed knowledge illusory.[11] Revelation is the basis for *all* knowledge of God. In fact, the "whole world-process" offers knowledge of God.

This statement becomes clearer when Temple's use of Whitehead's philosophy is recognized. All existence is composed of various levels of reality—matter, life, mind, spirit; each level, which is necessary to the actuality of the next higher level, finds its own meaning and completion through being used by the higher.[12] The highest level is the principle of unity pervading and directing the whole. The "principle" is God, and God is personal. *"But Personality is always transcendent in relation to Process."*[13] God is thus transcendent, but he manifests himself as immanent in the process through which he achieves the purposes of his divine volition.

This, then, is the reason Temple sees the possibility of a natural knowledge of God. What man sees in nature, in all existence, in the movements of history, is God's "conduct," his self-expression. It becomes apparent why Temple should consider general revelation essential to special revelation. The fact that it is God who acts means that he can use either uniform or unique processes to reveal himself, for he "acts on each occasion as is appropriate for the fulfillment of the divine purpose."[14] His "specially adapted activities" are most "fully revelatory"[15] and constitute specific revelation. That revelation, it has been seen, culminates in Jesus Christ. But all revelation, whatever the form, springs from the fact that personality "exhibits itself supremely in purposes of fellowship or love,"[16] and that God's self-revelation seeks to draw finite spirits into fellowship with him.

"Revelation so conceived is the full actuality of that relationship between Nature, Man and God,"[17] Temple says, and so indicates something of his gigantic effort to express "in conceptual terms what is nothing less than life itself."[18] It is his holding together in an organic whole the eternal and the historical, spirit and matter, which enables him to see the whole universe as sacramental of God himself to his creatures.

Revelation and the Word of God: Karl Barth

Barth's doctrine of revelation is basic to his monumental theological system developed in his *Church Dogmatics*. To say that the theology Barth propounds is above all a theology of the Word of God is to indicate something of the kind of role he holds as leader of those who center everything in God's action in self-revelation to persons granted by him the conditions for receiving this revelation. For Barth, revelation signifies "the Word of God itself, the act of its utterance," and there is "nothing other, nothing higher above this act from which it might be based or derived."[19] It has been suggested that actually, for Barth, revelation describes *"the whole of the existential relationship in which man is confronted by God."*[20] In order to understand how, within this context, revelation is viewed as the Word of God, it is necessary to be more specific.

The Forms of the Word of God

The threefold form of the Word of God is the Preached Word, the Written Word, and the Revealed Word; or church proclamation, the Holy Scripture, and Jesus Christ.

The Preached Word. In the event of real proclamation, man's word of witness to the Word of God is responded to in faith, and thus becomes God's Word to man; thus the church becomes the church, for this proclamation is her life-function. Not in any sense, however, does the faith-response of the person who hears the preached word make that word into the Word of God. Nor does the preacher's intention that these words shall become the Word, nor his efforts, nor any man-made factor become the determining element. Indeed, the preacher is placed in a dilemma. He has been commanded by God to speak, yet he knows that when he speaks, it is but a human word and will remain a human word. But he sees the possibility, he knows that in God's own free and contemporary act, God may speak his Word. And man knows that he is to speak in obedience to the Word, that he is to seek diligently to understand, that he is to remember that the gospel "is as responsible for those who proclaim it as for those to whom it is proclaimed."[21] His work can be done only in humility and in hope.

Furthermore, a responsibility is laid upon all members of the church to study and seek to interpret the Bible, not leaving this task to scholars and preachers only. Although Barth does not say so, perhaps there is a real implication for Christian education in his view that "the Word of God has surrendered itself so fully to the need of interpretation that some mediation is always necessary."[22] The church *as a whole* exists to carry on this mediatorial work.

The Written Word. The written witness to revelation, the Bible, calling, guiding, empowering the church in her proclamation, may, by its "imposition of itself on the strength of its special content,"[23] also be found to be the Word of God. It is thus necessary to distinguish the Bible as such from revelation; a witness is not to be identified with that to which it witnesses. On the other hand, it must be affirmed in the same moment that there *is* a sense in which the witness is a unity with revelation. How can both these things be true? Because revelation "accommodates" itself to man, being mediated through human words which remain human words, and yet which become a unity with the revelation which is "the basis, object, and content" of the words. The fact that a fallible, human word can become God's Word and yet retain its own identity is a paradox, a miracle of God's freedom.[24]

The Revealed Word. Scripture attests to the objective fact of revelation that has taken place in Jesus Christ, through its account of the expectation and recollection of that event. Man is confronted by "the singular Word spoken, and this time really directly, by God Himself."[25] Revelation is therefore an objective actuality in Jesus Christ, a once-for-all event, but it is also that which occurs over and over again in history, as men, confronted by God, are constituted in their very existence, brought into being as new creations through the subjective actuality of the work of the Holy Spirit.

The preached, the written, the revealed Word, are not three clearly distinguishable forms. There is a unity in this threeness comparable to the unity-in-threeness of the Trinity. They are so interrelated as to be interdependent, as to be *one* Word of God. The Father, the Son, the Spirit, are all modes of being of the Reality of God. In each mode, God is truly God, yet no single form can account for the others. Revelation, designating one act which is yet threefold, is thus the basis for the doctrine of the Trinity. It is necessary to see this interdependence in order to understand the relation between God and man, or between God as Absolute and as accommodating himself to men, or between God as Subject and as Creator of the ground for the reception of his act.

The Content of the Word of God

The nature of revelation, its content, cannot be seen apart from the forms, for form "is obviously always the form of a content."[26] From what has already been said, the deduction might be drawn that it would be sufficient to say the content of revelation is God himself. It is *self*-revelation, and the Word is the Word of *God*. Immediately it must be recalled that the revelation is of the Triune God, as Creator, Reconciler, Redeemer; as Father, Son, Spirit. Just to say that there is a personal disclosure is therefore misleading. The disclosure is not of the attributes of some personality, but of the *Word* of God. That means God speaks, God acts, he reveals himself to men. And in every confrontation of man, God's entire being, speaking, acting, interpret for man the *meaning* of the content of revelation, at the same time that he remains a Mystery, in his veiling and his unveiling. The hearing of the real Word of God, not possible to man, is the work of the Spirit, who enables man, through faith, to perceive meaning within mystery. It is the veiling which is an unveiling, the union of form and content in mystery which is miracle.

Two somewhat prosaically practical questions arise shortly. If this is the content of revelation, what is the importance of specific situations and acts of individuals as recorded in the Bible? What is the role of words, of simple, human words, in relation to revelation? The answers to both are implied in what has been said, but the questions are of such concern in the field of Christian education that they need to be made more explicit. Barth speaks directly to both.

As to the first, it must be pointed out that the Bible is a historical book, and must be understood historically. This is a demand which the Bible itself posits, Barth says, one which must be taken seriously. What it means is taking the Bible for what it undoubtedly is and is meant to be: "the human speech uttered by specific men at specific times in a specific situation, in a specific language and with a specific intention."[27] Any understanding which is dependable must be one which has honestly taken these factors into consideration. The kind of truth which is aimed at man's existence, and which comes to him in particularities, can never be found in generalized statements of abstract truth, Barth says. This does not mean that, in general conceptual terms, men are not to repeat and anticipate what God has said and says; it only means that man must remember that his reflections are his own work, and that God may speak to different individuals in quite different ways. It would suggest, too, that in these specific historical situations where God has acted, men throughout the centuries find a continuing point of reference for the understanding of their own lives, events which are better as permanent points of reference than their own experiences, so subject to fluctuations of time and situation.

And the words of the Bible? They cannot be discarded so lightly as a too spiritual or too existential approach to the Bible would do.

> If God speaks to man, He really speaks the language of this concrete human word of man. That is the right and necessary truth in the concept of verbal inspiration. If the word is not to be separated from the matter, if there is no such thing as verbal inspiredness, the matter is not to be separated from the word, and there is real inspiration, the hearing of the Word of God, only in the form of verbal inspiration, the hearing of the Word of God only in the concrete form of the biblical word.[28]

There is, then, a verbal inspiration, but not an infallible biblical word. It is an inspiration which permits faulty human words to be used by God, to become his Word. Man's role is not to imagine that the Word of God is present in the biblical text, nor to use any devices to make it present, for man has no responsibility for distinguishing the divine from the human, for separating words into more valuable and less valuable. God may choose any words with any persons to become his Word. Man's responsibility is to be persistent in waiting and knocking, to accept the concrete form of the biblical text as a challenge to concrete effort.[29]

The Knowability of the Word of God

There can be no question about the knowability of the Word of God. He is known, therefore he is knowable. In his freedom he has chosen to be known, and has given man in his human freedom the possibility of this knowledge. The knowledge which comes to man through the work of the Holy Spirit may be defined as "that confirmation of human acquaintance with an object whereby its trueness becomes a determining factor in the existence of the man who knows."[30]

It is precisely this knowledge which, determining man in the totality of his self-determination, may be known as experience. So, in this sense, experience of the Word of God is possible. But, although knowledge and experience of the Word of God are possible for man, there is nothing *in* man himself which makes this possible. There is no *analogia entis,* but an *analogia fidei.* From within faith, made possible by the Holy Spirit working within man, there comes the possibility of a knowledge of God. Faith is both an act of man, and the condition created by God for the reception of his self-revelation.

The Authority of the Word of God

An understanding of the nature of the Word of God as revelation is the answer to the question of authority. Authority rests in the Word by virtue of its content. It is God's Word, and constitutes itself its own authority, guaranteed by no higher authority because it is itself unconditional. This cannot be proved, only confessed. It cannot be controlled, only obeyed. All mediate, relative human authorities—those of the Bible, the church, confessional statements of the church, church teachers—all these derive their authority from the Word, witnessing to that Word by which they are constituted and communicating power for response. The recognition of authority in the attestation to revelation is as much God's work as is revelation itself, so that, in the final analysis, authority rests in the actuality of the Triune God.

But authority is not to be understood apart from freedom. Indeed, it is in essence but God's freedom for man. And insofar as

God makes possible man's freedom for Him, that is, insofar as God creates a freedom for obedience, authority as man comes to know it is related to his own freedom.

Man and the Bible

Man's freedom under the Word carries with it a responsibility for asseveration in the confession of the glory of God and for the persistent effort to interpret and apply Holy Scripture. Members of the church can never be spectators or even objects of the governing of the church by the Scripture, nor can they sit and wait passively for the church to call them and effect for them participation in its life. The miracle is that human words always need interpretation; thus is given to men the possibility for being included in the revelational event.

The Word of God which can speak clearly to man and yet never gives itself completely to human interpretation must be approached with the spirit of a free subordination of all human ideas and convictions to the divine witness in the Scripture. That is behind the quite concrete tasks necessary for interpretation, which are identified by Barth in three stages.

The first is the act of *observation*. Reminding oneself of the nature of the Word, one seeks to see the words as documents of concrete historical situations through literary-historical investigation, and thereby to form an idea of what is really said in the text. It is an effort to form an accurate picture (placed properly in the context of the series of pictures of which it is a part) of the real situation and its meaning for those who participated in it.

The second stage is the act of *reflection*. It is not an act which follows the first in time, but is to be seen as the "one act of scriptural exegesis considered now in the moment of the transition of what is said into the thinking of the reader or hearer. We are now just at the middle point between *sensus* and *usus, explicatio* and *applicatio*."[31] It is the process by which the reader comes to "accompany" that which is written. He begins to see himself in relation to what has happened, and realizes that he cannot free himself from "his own shadow," from the system of thought, the epistemology, he brings with him. He must recognize these facts, and use his own orientation, methods, skills, in a critical way, in conscious subordination to the Word in exegesis.

The third stage is *appropriation,* again not a separate act but only a moment in the "one totality of scriptural interpretation."[32] Now the men who interpret become *conscientes,* "co-knowers," assimilating what has been said into their own inner impulse, so that it becomes a fundamental orientation of their whole existence. This never means that there will emerge a general theory that man may consider and apply in separate acts, a procedure which Barth characterizes as the "unholy doctrine of 'theory and practice.' "[33] It has to do with a word spoken to a particular person, where it is assimilated in accordance with what he is like. This is possible not because he "stubbornly insists on trying to know for himself in what everything will consist if it is imparted to him,"[34] nor because he centers attention on his own concerns and questions. Precisely because he allows himself to be lifted out of himself into the concerns and questions of the situation depicted in the words of the Bible can light fall upon his own life.

Is this to say, then, that men find in the Bible "what they are to do"? The answer is both "yes" and "no." It is "no" if men expect there a simple list of things to do and not to do. It is "yes" if it is recognized that the Bible must be understood in relationship to revelation, that revelation brings to men the possibility of existence as Christians, and that what men do is related to what men are. As men are confronted by the Word they come to exist through the power of the Spirit and to respond in free acts of decision. For Barth, as for Calvin, the life of the Christian is a life of gratitude. "It is in this praise of God that the children of God live, who love God, because He first loved them."[35]

Revelation and Reason: Paul Tillich

If Barth stands as the great representative of a theology of *diastasis,* Tillich stands as the great representative of a theology of *synthesis*. But this is not the liberal synthesis, with its concept of continuity which blurred the distinction between man and God; it is not eclecticism, nor the merging of definable ideas. Rather, it is holding them together in proper tension, as Tillich, in the role of mediating theologian, endeavors to do with philosophy and theology. Here is no disparagement of either reason or revelation. Tillich's emphasis on ontology points to a closeness to essentialism, although his concern with knowledge "in which the very existence of the knower himself is involved"[36] points to an influence from existentialism. It is the knowledge which comes through revelation which is the answer to the human being's plea to hear the answer to his question, "What is the meaning of existence?" The section entitled "Reason and Revelation" is thus logically placed as Part I of Tillich's *Systematic Theology*, but it is necessary to consider this in connection with other phases of his thought in order to understand his epistemological position and the meaning he attaches to revelation.

Theology and Philosophy

The theologian speaks from within the Christian church and carries out a function of the church. That function is to satisfy two basic needs, "the statement of the truth of the Christian message and the interpretation of this truth for every new generation."[37] If theology is to speak to the present situation, it cannot escape a consciousness of movement and meaning in history, of the "living import" within cultural forms. Thus Tillich's emphasis on culture and history. If the theologian is to analyze and articulate that meaning, to state the questions implied in the human situation, and then to express the answers in thought-forms understandable for the contemporary man, he cannot escape philosophy. Philosophy therefore plays a crucial role in the relating of revelation to man.

The Method of Correlation

The method which Tillich advocates is one which he says systematic theology has always used to some degree, more or less consciously. Perhaps this is because a method which serves its true function of providing "a way around" is one which is not decided upon a priori, but is being decided continually in the cognitive process itself. If it is adequate to the subject matter, it arises out of an effort to understand that subject matter, and awareness of the method being employed follows the application of the method, never precedes it. Method is of tremendous importance because it is so organically interwoven with content that it becomes "an element of the reality itself," and method and system "determine each other."[38]

The method of correlation helps explain Tillich's understanding of the Christian faith. Existential questions and theological answers are mutually interdependent, primarily because, as Tillich says, the answers which come through revelation have meaning only when "they are in correlation with questions concerning the whole of our existence, with existential questions."[39]

Consider the nature of these answers.

> The Christian message provides the answers to the questions implied in human existence. These answers are contained in the revelatory events on which Christianity is based and are taken by systematic theology *from* the sources, *through* the medium, *under* the norm.[40]

The *sources* are the Bible, church history, and the history of religion and culture; the *medium* is experience; the *norm* is the New Being, manifest in Jesus the Christ. This norm, which arises from "the encounter of the church with the Christian message,"[41] differs from one period to another. In the Reformation, for example, the norm was "justification by faith," arising out of the church's concern about the forgiveness of sins and the mercy of God. Today, out of man's question about his self-estrangement, his separation from the ground of being, arises the question concerning "a reality of reconciliation and reunion, of creativity, meaning, and hope."[42] Jesus as Christ, the New Being, *is* this reality, this hope, and he is the norm for revelation today.

Revelation and Its Correlation with Reason

If Tillich follows his designated method, it should be possible to see in the cognitive structure of reason that which calls for and correlates with revelation. Such is the case. The five statements offered here should help make this clear, and define revelation.

First, there is a correlation between the structure of the human mind and the structure of reality which makes it possible for human reason to have a knowledge of reality, a knowledge which solves the conflicts within human reason and reunites it to the ground of being at the same time. This structure is to be found in ontological reason, rather than technical reason, and has both a subjective side (mind) and an objective side (world). The structure of reason points to its own depth—the cognitive realm to truth-itself, the aesthetic realm to beauty-itself, the legal realm to justice-itself, the communal realm to love-itself. In any of these realms, where reason is actualized, there is always movement, life, the possibility of creativity, a tension between the static and the dynamic.

It should be pointed out here that technical reason does have a role to play in the understanding of the Christian faith. It is an instrument, the "capacity for reasoning," and refers to a means-ends relation, accepting "ends" from elsewhere, and seeking to determine appropriate means. When it becomes the only kind of reason employed in the field of theology, it is dangerous. God becomes a "thing," religion a superstition, and a dichotomy is established between reason and revelation. On the other hand, when technical reason is the companion of ontological reason, as indicated above, the dichotomy is overcome, technical reason becomes an instrument for "establishing a consistent, logical, and correctly derived organism of thought."[43] This is Tillich's approach to a solution to the role of reason, one of the major theological issues today.

Second, although one recognizes "the *logos* structure of the grasping-and-shaping self and the *logos* structure of the grasped-and-shaped world,"[44] he sees that the ambiguities within human reason itself prevent a proper relation between the two. The tension between structure and depth, in reason, produces a conflict between autonomy and heteronomy; reason may affirm and actualize its structure without considering its relation to reality, or it may respond to strange commands from outside. The tension between the static and dynamic element in every rational process produces the conflict in existence between the absolute and the relative. The tension between the formal and the emotional elements produces the conflict between formalism and irrationalism. In every case, the conflict calls for and points to that which "answers" it in revelation.

Third, revelation is defined as "the manifestation of something hidden which cannot be approached through ordinary ways of gaining knowledge,"[45] or as "the manifestation of what concerns us ultimately."[46] There is "no reality, thing, or event which cannot become a bearer of the mystery of being and enter into a revelatory correlation."[47] Nature, history, groups, individuals, the word, all may be media of revelation. But no medium has revelatory power in itself; such a claim is idolatry. Only as it points beyond, becomes "transparent to the ground of being," does it mediate revelation. If it seems, then, that Tillich sees a general revelation, it is to misunderstand him, although he does see revelation as being universal in intention. It is always existential, always occurs in particular situations. It has its subjective side (religion) and is an objective event. "There is no revelation if there is no one who receives it as his ultimate concern."[48] That is why revelation is always "special revelation."

Original and dependent revelation are to be distinguished from each other. "An original revelation is a revelation which occurs in a constellation that did not exist before."[49] On the other hand, "In a dependent revelation the miracle and its original reception together form the giving side, while the receiving side changes as new individuals and groups enter the same correlation of revelation."[50]

Fourth, although there is a correlation between subjective and objective reason, the human mind cannot of itself grasp the reality with which it is confronted. It is only as Being manifests itself—never losing its mystery—through a miracle, or, better, through *sign-events,* that the reason, confronted with a kind of "ontological shock," responds in an ecstasy which does not destroy the rational structure of the mind, but carries the mind beyond itself. This revelatory knowledge is self-validating, somewhat in the way a mystical experience is self-validating, but different from mysticism in that it also validates itself in the life process.

The knowledge of revelation, which is also knowledge of God, is always symbolic. The only non-symbolic statement is that God is Being-Itself. Symbols (to be distinguished from signs, which are "consciously invented and removed"[51]) point beyond themselves, participate in that to which they point, but are not to be identified with it, and are born out of a situation, dying when the reality to which they point no longer exists. Moreover, their main function is "the opening up of levels of reality which otherwise are hidden and cannot be grasped in any other way."[52]

Fifth, Jesus as the Christ is the final revelation. He is the center of history for those to whom he reveals himself. He is the New Being. He, rather than the Bible, is the norm for all revelation. "Christian theology affirms that he is all this because he stands the double test of finality: uninterrupted unity with the ground of his being and the continuous sacrifice of himself as Jesus to himself as the Christ."[53]

Observe the relevance of this to each of the three conflicts of reason-in-existence. The answer to the conflict between autonomy and heteronomy is theonomy, where reason becomes transparent to its own depth. In the conflict between the absolute and the relative, the answer is Jesus as the Christ, who, in the concreteness of his personal life, is the bearer of that which is absolute. The answer to the conflict between formalism and irrationalism is Jesus as the Union of Form and Mystery.

Revelation and the Bible

The basic source for the theologian's explanation of the content of the Christian faith is the Bible, but this is not the only source. That has already been indicated, and Tillich decisively rejects the "assertion of neo-orthodox biblicism that the Bible is the *only* source,"[54] because the biblical message "cannot be understood and could not have been received had there been no preparation for it in human religion and culture."[55] Having made this point, Tillich is free to clarify the role of the Bible. It is basic because "it is the original document about the events on which the Christian church is founded."[56] Yet it is more than "original document." The fact that it contains the witness of persons responding to historical happenings which thereby became for them a participation in original revelation means that the Bible "is both original event and original document; it witnesses to that of which it is a part."[57] Moreover, persons drawn into a response to these events, to the biblical message, come to participate through the Bible in a dependent revelatory experience.

The Bible is in part a norm for the use of all sources—but only insofar as the encounter of its message with the ultimate concerns of each generation produces a norm by which the Bible itself, and all other sources, are to be studied for the answers they give to man's questions. This norm is not produced intentionally; it emerges out of the situation, and is recognized through the painstaking work of the philosopher-theologian. It is not a private opinion, because it is formulated in the church, the "place of work," where the church's life and collective experience become formative influences.

Another issue has to do with the relation of the Bible and the Word of God. Tillich sees different meanings for the term "Word of God," and concludes that probably "nothing has contributed more to the misinterpretation of the biblical doctrine of the Word than the identification of the Word with the Bible."[58] Nor can the Word be identified with the church's proclamation. Any part of life may become the situation in which the Word becomes real for a person, and "the mediator of revelation may not be a preacher or religious teacher at all but simply someone whom we meet and whose words become the Word for us in a special constellation."[59] This may be said, therefore, about the meaning of the Word of God:

> The many different meanings of the term "Word" are all united in one meaning, namely, "God manifest"—manifest in himself, in creation, in the history of revelation, in the

final revelation, in the Bible, in the words of the church and
her members. "God manifest"—the mystery of the divine
abyss expressing itself through the divine Logos—this is the
meaning of the symbol, "Word of God."[60]

Briefly, with respect to the authority of the Bible, it may be
said that the Bible is not the sole authority, nor the chief of a
hierarchy of authorities. Rather, authority rests in an interactive
process in which the Bible becomes a "message" for an individual
or the church only through the "experiencing participation of
the church and of every Christian."[61]

Because Tillich relates revelation to reason as well as to the
Bible, to philosophy as well as to Jesus the Christ, he has sometimes been accused of explicating some faith other than the Christian. As he sees it, however, there is no conflict between biblical
religion and the philosophical quest for ultimate reality. The
question of God arises on the level of existential being because
man is finite, because there is in him a tension between the drive
toward the infinity of being, of actualizing the potentialities
within, and the constant threat in nonbeing. He seeks the "really
real" at deeper and deeper levels "to a point where we cannot
speak of level any more, where we must ask for that which is the
ground of all levels, giving them their structure and their power
of being."[62] The answer to man's questioning finitude is the
ground of being, Being-Itself. This is the same thing as the biblical assertion that "God is." *Being* and *person* are not contradic-
tory concepts. The symbol "personal God" is "absolutely fundamental" as an expression of God's relatedness to man. Thus biblical personalism becomes a unity with ontology in the doctrine
of God, and revelation can be separated neither from the Bible
nor from philosophy.

Revelation and Encounter: Emil Brunner

Of primary concern here is Brunner's emphasis on the personal element in the encounter between God and man which, for
him, constitutes revelation. Certain other phases of his thought

may be noted, as dealing with issues raised by other writers, although it is not possible to consider in detail his extensive treatment of the doctrine of revelation.

Like Barth, Brunner sees that biblically revelation "always
meant the whole of the divine activity for the salvation of the
world, the whole story of God's saving acts."[63] These "saving acts"
are seen as "divine-human" encounters, a point of view Brunner
developed first in his *The Divine-Human Encounter,* published
in America in 1943. It is a point of view which he considers decisive for theology, and which he develops further in his *Dogmatics.* Although the idea is biblically oriented, it contains a truth
recognized elsewhere. Brunner says this: "The discovery of the
'I-Thou' truth in philosophy by Ebner and Buber is indeed, as
Heim has put it, a 'Copernican turning-point' in the history of
thought."[64] The "I-Thou truth" is seen as eventuating in "liberation from the rigidity and ethical sterility of orthodoxy" through
a faith "which is based on nothing save the Love of God revealed
in Jesus Christ."[65] This view of the personal character of faith
as encounter with the living Christ is seen as a rediscovery of a
Reformation truth, one which is wholly derived from the Bible.
As the key emphasis of Brunner's doctrine of revelation, it needs
further consideration.

The Word of God

The living Christ, the Word become flesh, is "the centre of
the divine manifestation." He is the Word of God, the "divine
self-communication." More than words about God, the Word is
"a Person, a human being, the man in whom God Himself meets
us."[66] In him all the complex forms of revelation are welded into
a unity. Yet he cannot be understood only in terms of "an isolated Fact," because there is a "before" and an "afterwards."[67]

The promises of the Old Covenant, the "before," are to be understood against the background of "the broken relationship between man and God," and point to fulfillment in Jesus Christ.[68]
The historical fact of Jesus Christ is to be understood also in
relationship to an "afterwards," for the revelation in him is ac-

cessible to future generations only through the New Testament teaching, which itself comes through the witness of the teaching church and of the Holy Spirit. And if the word "revelation" is to have its "full weight," a Christian of today must "look beyond 'the Word made flesh' to a future form of revelation, when we shall no longer merely 'believe,' but we shall 'see,' face to face."[69] In the "perfected revelation at the end of the ages," in the *Parousia*, "where all that separates has been removed, and where the fullness of the Presence has been realized," the meaning of revelation will be fully achieved.[70]

The I-Thou Relation

What happens when God takes the initiative in revealing himself, acting in history in a relationship to man of Lordship and fellowship? God reveals himself as Person, standing "over against" man as a "Thou." And something happens to man. *"An encounter takes place between God and man.* While God is coming to meet man He also makes possible man's going to meet Him."[71] It is in this encounter that revelation occurs as "a life-giving and a life-renewing communion."[72]

It is therefore the "I-Thou" relation alone which gives to man the dignity and responsibility of being a person. Moreover, it is only in such a context that men may become a "thou" to one another. The whole of the relationship among the people of God stems from this awareness of standing before God as subject, with his will to fellowship not only with individuals but with the community of men who freely respond to his love with love.

Something else happens in this encounter. Man cannot face the sovereign Lord who, in holy love, stands over against him, without becoming aware of his creatureliness, of his sinful nature (not just his sins) . The knowledge of God as Creator and the knowledge of self as creature are correlative truths. This self-understanding comes most clearly in God's personal revelation in Jesus Christ, who "leads us back to our home."[73]

And this "home-coming" is an overcoming of isolation, a surrendering of self in utter dependence on God, a faith which is a "trust-in-obedience," and an existence in responsibility. It is, indeed, a covenant relationship. Brunner cites approvingly Eichrodt's concept of an Old Testament theology based on the "Covenant relation,"[74] and sees here a truth which both biblically and throughout the history of the church has been constitutive of the Christian relation to God. A righteous and sovereign God who has covenanted with his people demands obedience from them. But because he wills communion, because he "takes fellowship seriously" and "cares for the human 'Thou,' "[75] his love desires a responsive love and an "obedience of faith." This concept of the I-Thou relation as the basis for the ethical life is of great significance for Christian education.

Furthermore, it is within the divine-human encounter, which is in part made possible through the Bible, that the authority of the Bible becomes effective. This authority rests upon encounter with the Christ of Scriptures. "We are not required to believe the Scriptures because they are the Scriptures; but because Christ, whom I am convinced in my conscience is the Truth, meets me in the Scriptures—therefore I believe."[76] In this Christocentric concept of authority, Brunner seems to have more in common with Luther than with Calvin.

Revelation and Reason

Like Barth, Brunner develops a doctrine of revelation which begins with the Bible, and which he believes to be consistent with the Bible. For both men, revelation is God's self-disclosure in Christ with the Bible as authoritative witness. Even within this general statement there are differences. But when the subject of the relationship between revelation and reason is approached, the divergence between the two thinkers develops to the point of controversy, and Brunner is to be understood at many points as being closer in thought to William Temple than to Karl Barth.

There are, for example, many points of agreement between Brunner and Temple with reference to the role of reason in recognizing and understanding general revelation, which is God's revelation in creation. It must be pointed out, however, that although there is a revelation in creation, for Brunner there is no such thing as natural theology.[77] Natural theology exists in the human effort to arrive at knowledge of God through speculative thought, but no valid knowledge is possible through such an approach. On the other hand, what God makes known in creation is available to all men, although it cannot be understood aright because of man's sin. What God grants to man in creation is the quality which makes him human. Thus there is that within man which serves as a point of contact between man and God, an *analogia entis;* man has been so created that he is capable of receiving God's revelation.

In part, this means that reason has a role to play in human life irrespective of revelation. God has designated a sphere of things, the world and the things of the world, which is "the legitimate sphere of reason."[78] These things man can know aright.

But natural knowledge is not saving knowledge. Salvation comes through revelation, and reason has a role to play as the counterpart of revelation. Reason has to do with the communication and appropriation of revelation. Brunner is convinced that each theologian must communicate with his generation through an understanding and use of philosophical terms with which people are conversant, even though theology is not derived from philosophy.

At an even deeper level, reason is essential to revelation. In a sense, it may be understood as the subjective side of the objective fact of revelation. Just as faith is necessary for the reception of the revelation in Christ, so reason is necessary for the reception of the revelation in creation—a reason enlightened through encounter with God in Christ to the point of perceiving the revelatory aspects of creation.

Reference to the subjective and objective aspects of revelation leads again to mention of an affinity of Brunner with Temple. Temple speaks of the "coincidence of event and appreciation"; Brunner says that revelation must be understood and received before it can be truly revelation, for "the reality of the revelation culminates in the 'subject' who receives it."[79] What Brunner seems to have done in his recognition of the human subjective aspect of revelation, which is integral to the "encounter" concept, is to recapture some of the experiential aspects of Temple's liberalism and to combine this understanding with certain neo-Reformation emphases found in more recent theological thought.

Revelation and *Metanoia:* H. Richard Niebuhr

Above all else, for Richard Niebuhr, revelation points beyond the relativity of man's understanding to the sovereign God whose understanding is *not* relative, and who, in his grace, reveals himself to man, thus drawing man into a great "drama of becoming," which is his response to God's continuing revelation. It is not a revelation which gives into man's possession "a book, a creed, or a set of doctrines."[80] That would be a static thing, and could not be the "revelation of a living God." What is meant, rather, is this:

> By revelation in our history, then, we mean that special occasion which provides us with an image by means of which all the occasions of personal and common life become intelligible. What concerns us at this point is not the fact that the revelatory moment shines by its own light and is intelligible in itself but rather that it illuminates other events and enables us to understand them.[81]

As man comes to view life from the perspective of this image— God's saving work for man—change is possible. In revelation, outer history becomes inner history. Historic experience leads to God. Reason becomes the servant of revelation. The self is converted, as ideas and behavior are continually transformed. Consider further these aspects of Niebuhr's understanding of revelation.

Inner and Outer History

Just as language conditions thought, just as word and ideas are inseparable, so is the internal history of a person or a group conditioned by external history. This is a key emphasis of Rich-

ard Niebuhr. There is no way a person can get out of the particular position he occupies in history to a realm beyond time-space,
so that he is able to observe past and future as impinging upon
the present, so that he sees and participates in the totality of
events and ideas as they stand in relation to one another and
to all other events and ideas. He cannot escape the vantage point
from which he views life. When he assumes that he can, when
he elevates his limited knowledge to a position of timeless, universally valid abstract truth, refusing to admit such knowledge
to have been conditioned by his own standpoint, his devotion
and commitment turn that which is relative into that which is
absolute, and his defense of his position draws self into the picture as central. It is, indeed, a refusal to accept one's finitude, to
recognize as valid the meaning in life as mediated through a
particular history. This means that the beginning point for the
Christian is the faith of the Christian community, because God
and faith belong together.

Applied to the preaching of the early Christian church, this
also explains why preaching was "primarily a simple recital of
the great events connected with the historical appearance of Jesus
Christ and a confession of what had happened to the community of disciples."[82] Was it not that "internal life does not exist
without external embodiment,"[83] and that these events-in-them-
selves became revelatory as his followers perceived their inner
meaning? Inner history is the sphere of revelation, but "faith is a
strange thing; it is not sufficient to itself and will not work
alone."[84] This faith which moves to God through historic experience is not an individualistic and mystical experience. The New
Testament evangelists "did not speak of events . . . as impersonally
apprehended, but rather of what had happened to them in their
community."[85] They looked at the past not as spectators but as
participants, so that the history of the church was viewed as "the
story of 'our fathers,' of 'our Lord,' and of the actions of 'our
God.' "[86]

Within the Christian community, then, where members can "re-
fresh as well as criticize each other's memories,"[87] revelation can

be verified by reason, and persons seeking to understand better the external history of the church are drawn to participate in its inner life, to become a community of selves bound to one another. The effort to interpret the external history of the church keeps it from exalting itself or its inner history, and calls it instead to repentance. Having seen God's hand at work in events in their own lives, Christians are reminded that he is at work in all events, of all times and places and persons, that he is the universal God. To seek unity in the multiplicity of events, to try to understand his ways of working with men through a "faithful external history" is to know him better. To look honestly at the external history of both self and church is to know better both God and self, and to approach partially and successively the knowledge of the inner and outer history of person and of community known simultaneously by God.

Revelation and Historic Faith

Granted that the way of faith in God is through historic experience, what is that historic event which serves as an "image" by which Christians interpret their lives? "The special occasion to which we appeal in the Christian church is called Jesus Christ, in whom we see the righteousness of God, his power and wisdom."[88] There is more to be said. "Revelation means God, God who discloses himself to us through our history as our knower, our author, our judge and our only savior."[89] The response in the revelatory moment, when "we know ourselves to be known from beginning to end,"[90] can be "realized in us only through the faith which is a personal act of commitment, of confidence and trust, not a belief about the nature of things."[91] It is only then that the revelatory image can make the past intelligible, can interpret the present, and can make apparent the potentiality of the future. It is only then that, suffering self-knowledge in the light of the knowledge of the Revealer, man can be changed.

It should be said that this event of Jesus Christ is far more than a great occasion which becomes a symbol for that which is repeated again and again in the deaths and resurrections of human experience. It does more than give rise to some general ideas by which man may interpret his experiences. The story the early Christians told "was not a parable which could be replaced by another; it was irreplaceable and untranslatable."[92] It had to do with "a unique sonship, a unique obedience, a single sacrifice."[93]

It is through the Bible that the memory of Jesus Christ becomes a possibility for the church. The historic events of Israel and of the New Testament church came to have meaning and unity through the labor of writers who, equipped with "the light of revelation," could employ "the reasoning heart" to understand the meaning of what had happened. Just as a neural system is essential to the memory of an individual, so the Bible and the rites of the institutional church are essential to the common memory of the church.[94]

The way Niebuhr relates revelation and historic faith enables him to speak directly to a question of particular concern to Christian educators, the matter of whether and how the Christian faith is communicable. Particularly is this true where revelation is seen to be the divine self-disclosure.

> It cannot be enough to say that in revelation we meet the divine self, for if this meeting is pure immediacy which does not provide us with truths about God it would remain incommunicable and unable to provide the reasoning heart with principles of understanding.[95]

What then is communicable? The events of the external history of the church—which, appropriated by a person through an act of faith, become his own history. The understanding of the nature and will of God from the point of view of the writers of Scripture—knowledge *about* God. The confessional "story of our life," which is not an apologetic for the superiority of Christianity—but only a confession of what has happened, and of the unity and purpose it has enabled one to see in human existence. The natural knowledge of God and the moral law—all knowledge as interpreted by the Christian revelation. These things are communicable and are somehow, in the divine Providence, related to revelation. But revelation itself is not communicable.

Christianity and Metanoia

Throughout this consideration of the meaning of revelation, what existed as a presupposition of all Niebuhr's thought has become increasingly apparent. Christianity itself, as a historic faith, can best be conceived of as *metanoia,* "permanent revolution," and revelation is of prime significance because it is that recurring event in Christianity which enables the revolution to become a reality.

> Revelation is not a development of our religious ideas but their continuous conversion. God's self-disclosure is that permanent revolution in our religious life by which all religious truths are painfully transformed and all religious behavior transfigured by repentance and new faith.[96]

Because revelation does not accomplish the work of conversion alone, but employs reason, a closer look at the relation of reason and revelation would be helpful. Revelation does not equip men "with truth in such measure that no further labor in historical and psychological searching is necessary."[97] It neither hands finished creeds into the possession of reason, allowing for dogmatism, nor does it declare all things unintelligible, calling for skepticism. Instead, "the heart reasons with the aid of revelation."[98] Just as revelation did not excuse the writers of Scripture from "painful thought," so today men are called to reason on the basis of revelation in order to illuminate contemporary life and find there the manner and purpose of God's continuing work in history.

Thus revelation is not continuous with the natural knowledge of God and of the moral law, but rather serves as their transformer. No divine decrees for moral living are given. But God's revelation is not only a meeting with him as person; it is a revelation through Moses, the prophets, Jesus, of knowledge *about* him, about his nature and will, which are relevant to the moral life. Moreover, there is a moral law "written on our hearts apart from revelation and on our statute books without the aid of Scriptures."[99] These seemingly disparate elements are brought together when it is seen that just because the revelation is of *God,* the moral law which is known takes on a new imperativeness. It is known "as the demand of one from whom there is no flight,"[100] and "its evermore extensive and intensive application becomes necessary."[101] What happens is a "republication of the moral law." Religious behavior is transformed by revelation as religious beliefs are transformed. "A revolutionary transvaluation occurs not in addition to the personal revelation but because of it."[102]

The Christianity which is *metanoia* is also salvation.

The Consensus on Revelation

The theological perspectives presented in this study might be considered a documentation of the earlier statement that a consensus on the meaning of revelation seems to have emerged in the present time. It has resulted in the dissolution of the traditional doctrine and in the slow formulation of a new synthesis, a process still under way. Divergence of opinion and individual nuances of thought are too valuable to be forgotten, but it is important to try to draw up generalizations about the agreement in this "point of view" in order to see more clearly the theological thinking contributory to the emerging philosophy of Christian education.

The five statements offered here may be considered a kind of analytical summary of the survey that has been made, an indication of the major areas of agreement about the meaning of revelation.

Revelation is essentially the self-disclosure of God

Whether the witness to God comes through the Bible, as with Barth, or whether any event, person, or thing may point to him, as with Tillich, the prime fact is that *God* as self takes the initiative in manifesting himself, offering himself in fellowship to his people. This basic insight, so pervasive in recent thinking, consistently points to the sovereign Lord who cannot be possessed or controlled. God who in his love and freedom gives himself to be known is not limited by the relative forms, the written or spoken word, the concrete shape of human events. Those relative forms do not determine the content, the reality of revelation, nor can they ensure its communication. That is the work of God the Holy Spirit. So God comes to be known as he is, but always in mystery, even in Jesus Christ. And Jesus Christ *is* the revelation of God.

Either in biblical times or afterwards, whenever God's people have seen that he offers himself, not truths or propositions, the basic fact of their existence has been established. They speak thereafter from within a relationship which is in itself a knowledge *of* God, which may be explicated as knowledge *about* God, and which determines the perspective from which they view his actions in and throughout history. They come to self-knowledge, knowing themselves to be known by God.

It is quite possible to misinterpret this personal meeting or "I-Thou" relationship in terms of "pure immediacy," and to lead people into expectations which cannot be fulfilled. The personal meeting concept, however, does not refer only to moments of intense awareness. The experiential element may be present, it is true. But it is not communion without communication. As God's nature and character are known, the response is an understanding of his *will* which demands decision. That decision, that act of obedience, is faith.

Revelation takes place through God's "mighty acts," events on the plane of history apprehended by faith as God's action

A continually astounding fact about the God of the Christian faith is that in his absolute sovereignty he uses the relativities of man's life and the particulars of man's experiences to make himself known. In fact, all that man knows is mediated to him through the concrete forms of historical existence and comes to him at the point he occupies in space and time. It is only as man perceives that God has acted throughout time in those concrete events of history to accomplish his salvation that events become revelatory. Historical events in themselves are not revelation.

Only when God's "mighty acts" are discerned as such is God's purpose accomplished. The Exodus was an event. But only as Moses was divinely led to see the action and purpose of God in that event, and to interpret to Israel the meaning he saw, was there revelation—or real deliverance. Men could refer to this climactic event in which God acted mightily for their salvation, seeing in lesser events the same intention of the same God, and looking toward the future when his purpose would be accomplished fully. All history moved toward its fulfillment in the event of Jesus Christ, in his life, death, and resurrection, perceived by faith to be what it was.

The knowledge in such perception is not "about salvation," but is itself salvation, for God's revelation is always salvation, both as judgment and as redemption. Men's reflections on those events and their meaning, formulated as the witness of the Christian community, constitute a content to be communicated to persons who take this "outer history" for their own story, and thus are drawn into a response to God who revealed himself then and continues to reveal himself in his acts for the salvation of man.

It is important that this historical aspect of God's revelation be considered, as well as the personal meeting aspect. There is no way to the inner meaning of events except through their outer forms; it therefore becomes the responsibility of the church to preserve and teach about those events and the faith that understood them, so that, through God's grace, they may again become revelatory. Moreover, the accumulated knowledge of God's will and action in the past may engender in the Christian community an awareness of his hand in the present, demanding obedience, guiding, judging, redeeming still.

Revelation, as God's confrontation of man within the covenant community, is determinative of man's existence

Biblically, revelation was addressed to the covenant community, not to an individual. Witnessing to one another about what God was doing in and for his people, men found themselves confronted by God in a way that affected them at the core of their existence.

The same is true in the new Israel, the church. Within the covenant relationship and the covenant community, men re-enact in the individual and group decisions of daily existence their obedient (or disobedient) response to God's self-revelation, which is a revelation of his will. They do this, not as means of gaining his favor, but because, as new creations, they work out in the particulars of all their doing the real meaning of who they are. This means that their life in the covenant community is one of mutual support and of a shared understanding of God's revealed will. Therefore it might be said, with Barth, that because the Word of God surrenders itself to the need for interpretation, the church exists for mediatorial work. But the church itself is not redemptive, nor is the Bible. Redemption is of God alone.

The ethical implications of this concept are of tremendous significance, and are reminiscent of Reformation emphases.

Reason, now assigned a new role, is not the basis for revelation, but instead helps make it intelligible

Reason is the servant of revelation, not its basis. This much is agreed. It may be a matter of the use of reason to understand general revelation and to interpret the meaning of experience, so that reason becomes an integral part of revelation, as with Temple. With Brunner, it is important to note the role reason plays in the appropriation of revelation. With Tillich, there is emphasis on the use of reason to correlate the proper philosophical questions with the theological answers. It may be that revelation emancipates reason, and with its aid effects continuous conversion of ideas and behavior, as with Niebuhr. Or it may be a disparagement of reason, more verbal than actual, by avowed Barthians who fail to see that for Barth, too, reason may become the servant of revelation when God restores in the man of faith the *imago dei* destroyed in the fall. It is at this point that there are divergent opinions and strong controversies.

Although there is obviously less consensus here than elsewhere, there is agreement that all knowledge is of God, but that only revelation is "saving knowledge" and that if there is "general revelation," its meaning is seen only from the faith perspective of "special revelation." The concern is to point to a revolutionary and unique faith, more discontinuous with other religions than continuous with them. It has to do with a religion in which one knows the truth by doing it. Revelation, as act, response, and reality, is the basis of that religion. But reason is indispensable, because Christianity is not a formless faith, and because revelation can be appropriated only with the aid of reason.

The Bible, as witness to and participant in the event of revelation, is of unique significance in the church and in the life of man

The rediscovery of the Bible was a key factor in the Reformation, as it is in the theological renascence of today. Revelation somehow centers in and yet transcends the Bible. The words themselves—human, fallible words—witness to the God who discloses himself; they record his revelatory acts. Through the Holy Spirit the words may become the Word. Yet the Word is Jesus Christ, the revelation of God; he is God incarnate. There is throughout an inextricability of the divine and human which suggests the way God works with man—the absolute in the relative, the divine content in the worldly form, but the sovereign freedom never limited. It is not the relative, the form, the fallible word, that has authority. That comes from God. The authority of the Bible therefore rests in its content, not in its words. Because of that, the Bible is the norm for the life of man and the church. Moreover, it is the only record of those ways in which God has worked with man in history. Above all, it witnesses to Jesus Christ. As the record of those events, it is the "neural memory" of the church.

There seems to be a divine purposiveness in the use of the written word to serve as source and norm of faith. The very concreteness of the form of the written word might be said to be a challenge to concrete effort on the part of man, and in itself to constitute a situation which becomes the occasion for confrontation.

But that is revelation. The Bible therefore participates in the *event* of revelation, and is inseparable from it.

There are other elements in the recent thinking about revelation, but these are key emphases. They indicate something of the comprehensiveness of the term as it is now used, and how integral it is considered to be to the totality of God's work of reconciliation and redemption. As now conceived, revelation is far removed from the earlier, seemingly simpler equating of the words of the Bible with revelation. Yet the profundity of meaning assigned to the concept of revelation has given an even deeper significance to the Bible.

From Higher Criticism to Biblical Theology

Parallel with the emergence of the new consensus on revelation and in an interaction of mutual influence with that development has been a modification of the historico-grammatical understanding of the Bible typified in Fosdick's *Guide to Understanding the Bible*. The role assigned by Eichrodt to this book, of summing up the prevailing views of that generation, has been assigned by Ernest Wright for the contemporary period to Bernhard Anderson's *Rediscovering the Bible*.[103] This change, which marks the end of an era in New Testament theology,[104] and the "death and rebirth of Old Testament theology,"[105] came about through a complex of factors. It may have been Albert Schweitzer's *The Quest of the Historical Jesus* (1906) which pushed higher criticism to its limits and found that no "liberal" Jesus ever existed. The eschatological perspective of Jesus tied him to first-century Judaism, and he was inseparable from the faith of the early Christian community. Was the answer skepticism or different presuppositions as to methodology? Or it may have been, as Clarence T. Craig says, that the movement had run into bankruptcy generally.[106] But it remains true that the "objective" historians of biblical scholarship were not all "enemies of the faith,"[107] and that the "historical approach to biblical literature is one of the great events in the history of Christianity and even of religion and human culture," a method that still has an important role to play.[108] And the change came about from positive as well as from negative factors. Research was invigorated, as systematic theology had been, by the recovery of the biblical tradition.[109]

Thus it is that Anderson's book and others like it reflect such current emphases already considered as God's initiative in self-revelation, the witness to that revelation in the Bible, the historical nature of the Christian faith, Jesus Christ as the Living Word, and the continuing call for decision as men encounter God through the Bible. Biblical scholars see an authority and relevance to the biblical revelation which point to the nature of the Bible as *Heilsgeschichte,* or the story of salvation. There are varying interpretations of the key to the unity of the Bible, or of ways in which *Heilsgeschichte* is related to human history, but there is a wide area of agreement. There seems to be a convergence of biblical scholarship and theological trends as represented in the consensus scholars have been able to reach on principles of biblical interpretation, as formulated at the Ecumenical Study Conference at Wadham College, Oxford, in 1949. Seven theological presuppositions are designated as necessary to correct interpretation.

(a) It is agreed that the Bible is our common starting point, for there God's Word confronts us ...

(b) It is agreed that the primary message of the Bible concerns God's gracious and redemptive activity for the saving of sinful man that he might create in Jesus Christ a people for himself. . . . an authoritative claim is placed upon man and he is called upon to respond in faith and obedience throughout the whole of his life and work. The law of love has always a binding and compelling hold upon us, and in it we encounter the inescapable will of God. . . .

(c) It is agreed that the starting point of the Christian interpreter lies within the redeemed community of which by faith he is a member.

(d) It is agreed that the centre and goal of the whole Bible is Jesus Christ. This gives the two Testaments a perspective in which Jesus Christ is seen both as the fulfilment and the end of the Law.

(e) It is agreed that the unity of the Old and New Testaments is not to be found in any naturalistic development, or in any static identity, but in the ongoing redemptive activity of God in the history of one people, reaching its fulfilment in Christ. Accordingly it is of decisive importance for hermeneutical method to interpret the Old Testament in the light of the total revelation in the person of Jesus Christ, the Incarnate Word of God, from which arises the full Trinitarian faith of the Church.

(f) It is agreed that allegorical interpretations which were not intended by the Biblical authors are arbitrary and their use may be a disservice to the proper recognition of Biblical authority. But Christian exegesis has been justified in recognising as divinely established a certain correspondence between some events and teachings of the Old and of the New Testament.

(g) It is agreed that, although we may differ in the manner in which tradition, reason and natural law may be used in the interpretation of Scripture, any teaching that clearly contradicts the Biblical position cannot be accepted as Christian.[110]

The way in which biblical scholars pose and deal with issues relating to the Bible demonstrates in itself that the days of an unadulterated higher criticism are over. There are those, it is true, who make a catchword of "historicism" and spend their time in negative reaction to the work of biblical specialists. But those men themselves, aware of the "deceptive myth of neutrality,"[111] and of the fact that "the only possibility of bringing history to life lies in . . . appropriating it from some definite standpoint,"[112] have in effect said this:

> We will not confine ourselves to historico-critical study of the Biblical texts; our study must be put at the service of the Christian proclamation. Thus we should restore that fruitful co-operation between the several theological disciplines (historical, systematic and practical theology) that for long enough has been lost. While exegetical work upon Scripture constantly recalls theology as a whole back to Scripture, it puts itself at the service of the other disciplines.[113]

There is the fear on the part of some that the new trend toward a theological interpretation of historical, archaeological, and sociological facts may lead to a tendency "to theologize without taking care to ascertain the data on which one's work must be built."[114] Or, as Harold Willoughby sees it, already "the gregarious habits of biblical students and scholars are impelling to an unbalanced overconcentration of effort in the single area of biblical theology."[115]

In spite of these cautions, emphasis on theological interpretation grows apace. James D. Smart says that biblical theology is "in the early stages of its development" and "should have its most interesting growth and fruition in the years directly ahead of us."[116] Some have gone so far as to suggest that biblical theology is the key discipline.[117]

Actually, the relationship between biblical and systematic theology is yet to be worked out, and the exact definition and limitations of biblical theology more clearly defined. It seems safe to say at this point in the movement from higher criticism to biblical theology that historical study and theological interpretation have not proven to be immiscible areas, and that what Cunliffe-Jones proposes as the proper relationship is already partly realized in practice. His principle is "that the historical study of the Bible and the theological study of it, though closely interrelated, are not the same, and that the greatest fruitfulness in Biblical studies lies in the constant interaction of these two divergent yet interdependent interests."[118]

This kind of interaction results in a biblical theology which is more than doctrine as such. It relates to the effort to understand the dynamic movement of the thought and life of people in response to God's actions upon and in them, and to express that movement not so much in terms of ideas as of interpretation of the meaning in events.

It is within this context and climate that the Christian educator is working today. Although he is concerned with these same theological questions and his primary loyalty is to the Christian faith, he has the problem of integrating insights from many disciplines and of working out through all the multifarious details of concrete plans worthy and effective forms—inseparable from the content—by which the gospel communicates itself. As he assumes his task, he is faced with four major issues relating to the role of the Bible in Christian education: the meaning of revelation; the nature of the biblical witness; the relevance of the Bible; the appropriation of the biblical message. How are these issues being dealt with in Christian education today?

III The Meaning of Revelation

The first issue to be considered, the meaning of revelation as interpreted in the context of Christian education—or, better, as providing the context *for* Christian education—is basic to the other three issues. *What* God makes known of himself, as well as the *way* he chooses for revelation, has implications for Christian education. Distinctive emphases of the three men in the contemporary educational field who have written most extensively on these implications are to be considered here. James Smart's position may be characterized by his emphasis on revelation and content, Randolph Crump Miller's by his on revelation and process, and Lewis J. Sherrill's by his on Christian education as a corollary of revelation.

Because these same writers have dealt also with the other three issues, the procedure in the three chapters following this one shall be to present the position of each of the writers, following the same order as in this chapter.

Revelation and the Content of Christian Education

The decisive thing about Christian education for James Smart is its content. Often the word "content" is used to designate subject matter, and even subject matter is seen as crucially important when it is recognized as being determined by revelation. If God has revealed himself to his people in history, then whatever points to that revelation in its continuing relevance—and nothing else—constitutes basic subject matter for Christian education. But to say that the content of Christian education is God's revelation

67

in Jesus Christ is far more significant. It is to say that Christian
education is determined by the very essence of that with which
it deals, or that the "content" of revelation "imposes itself as
such" upon the form and the process of Christian education. Because Christian education is under the control of revelation, its
foundation rests in the doctrine of the Trinity. It centers around
and is empowered by the continuing creative activity of the Word
of God. Its sphere of activity is the church. And its purpose is to
be a "servant of revelation." Thus man's role as educator is to be
understood only in the light of God's role as revealer. Consider
further the preceding statements.

The Doctrine of the Trinity: The Foundation of Christian Education

In his chief work on philosophy of Christian education, *The
Teaching Ministry of the Church*,[1] Smart takes as a starting point
the doctrine of the Trinity, and tries to show the implications of
this doctrine for the educational program of the church. This
beginning point is significant not only in its marked contrast to
an earlier religious education beginning with man's needs and
experiences but also in its reflection of a Barthian influence,
which appears rather consistently although not without modifications. Even the terminology used is often suggestive of Barth.
God reveals himself as Creator, Redeemer, and Reconciler. His
eternal action in revelation as he goes forth from himself in his
Word is for the redemption of the world. Because his Word is
inseparable from himself, "it cannot be received by men without
their receiving God into themselves as Spirit."[2] The prophets
knew this, for "when they heard the word of the Lord, it was
never merely a word about the Lord or a word from the Lord,
but rather, a Word in which the Lord himself confronted them
as a living presence before whom man could only bow in faith
and obedience."[3] In the fullness of time the Word came even
closer to man, incarnate in Jesus Christ, sharing in man's humanity and yet remaining God's Word. In his eternal nature
God is Father, Son, and Spirit. "The Trinity, therefore, is a de-

scription of how God comes to man, to sinful man, and yet remains the God that he is."[4]

In what way is this doctrine of significance for Christian education? Although Smart does not relate the whole of his philosophy and program to the doctrine of the Trinity in a way as systematic or explicit as might have been expected, he does specifically designate two important points which should be considered. The New Testament doctrine of the church, which is "the necessary outcome of the doctrine of the Trinity," is crucial in Christian education, both as foundation and as defining the goal.[5] The church comes into being because it is there that the redemptive purpose of revelation is fulfilled as men are fashioned into new creations. But men are not simply made anew one by one. "They are fashioned into a fellowship that is wholly at God's disposal and offers itself as a body to Jesus Christ to be used by him in the fulfillment of his redemptive purpose."[6] Christian education has no life and no purpose apart from this understanding of the church.

A second doctrine, that of justification by faith alone, is equally important and, as with Barth, is related to the doctrine of the Trinity. Nothing that man does or can do can secure his salvation. Man's becoming a Christian is an act of God's grace. The response of faith to God's act in Christ is the work of the Spirit, and "the new life that a man then begins to live is God's gift to him in each moment."[7]

In Smart's contention that education, to be Christian, must rest upon the doctrine of the Trinity, it becomes possible to see several specific implications for teaching. The Triune God can be known *only* through the biblical revelation. Smart takes his stand with Barth in rejecting the careless use of the word "revelation" to refer to all truth. The result is confusion when a second source of revelation is tolerated alongside Scripture. There is the *Christian* truth, which is revelation, and which is recorded in the Bible, not in nature or in conscience.[8] Experience can no more lead to nor prove the existence of God than can reason. Although there is a partial truth in the belief that the experience of salvation gives to man "the key which unlocks the mysteries of divine truth,"[9] there is also the possibility that this emphasis may lead to "an unhealthy and futile straining after an inner experience which we do not possess."[10]

Such a view points not only to the importance of the Bible but to the "God-centeredness" of the Christian faith. It has in it an implication concerning the role of an educator in a revealed religion. The sovereign God who reveals himself and makes possible the reception of that revelation in a response which is redemption is not under the control of any educational process, and knowledge of him is not dependent upon any activity of man. Witnessing to faith in this God who reveals himself is what man can do, for the truth that is God does its own work. Smart's conviction is that "if we would let God's truth loose among us, unchained and undistorted, we should soon see the changes coming about, both in the Church and in the world, which we so much desire."[11] Note again the emphasis on *content* as the determining factor in Christian education.

There follows from this another implication. Lest it witness to a false faith, Christian education must ally itself with theology, which is the church's way of mounting "the watchtower" and scanning "its life and faith in all directions, in order to detect the presence of blindness, unbelief, unfaithfulness, and sin, and give warning before it is too late."[12] The peril to the church does not come from without but from within. Because of the truth which is its life, the church is invulnerable to outside powers so long as it is a faithful church.

Christian education, therefore, must not carry on its work as "nothing more than a study of educational psychology and techniques."[13] It is "more than methodological addenda to the curriculum."[14] In the practical department, it is a theological discipline along with biblical, systematic, and historical disciplines. Doubtless Barth might raise some questions with Smart at this point. After six years as editor in chief of the Presbyterian Faith and Life curriculum, the theologian Smart was enough influenced by his own role as educator to see the "involvement of Christian education in the total structure of theology."[15] He could say with conviction that "the teacher of the Word requires the same grounding Biblically, systematically, and historically, as the preacher of the Word."[16]

The Ministry of the Word of God

To say that the Christian educator's role, like the preacher's, is a ministry of the Word is to say that both point to God's unique revelation of himself in history, witnessed to in the Bible, and to the fullness of his revelation in Jesus Christ, confronting man in judgment and mercy. In both Old and New Testaments God's self-revelation is a creative act. What he led Moses to understand of his purpose in that supremely important event of the Exodus became determinative for the future of Israel. His revelation was in itself the creation of the covenant relationship which constituted Israel as God's people and gave them a unique destiny. The understanding Israel came to have of God's will and purpose through his saving acts in history was a revelation of God himself, fulfilled in Jesus Christ, the living Word.[17] God's revelation of himself is always a revelation of man, and therefore always confrontation, demanding decision. "The man who has no knowledge of God can have no knowledge of sin,"[18] for, as Smart says, right understanding of self and destiny comes to man only in the light of God's presence. That right understanding and the power to change come in Jesus Christ. God's creating, redeeming power continues to come to man through his word. What, then, about man's responsibility for teaching?

> We may sum up the entire consideration by saying that, in both Old and New Testaments, the word of God in which God reveals himself and in revealing himself comes to man for his salvation, requires two services primarily of those who respond to it: first, that they should preach this word that has come to them, and secondly, that they should teach it.[19]

Teaching and preaching are not to be identified, according to Smart, although the *content* of the two is the same. "It is the same Jesus Christ who is to be taught and who is to be preached."[20] Preaching, however, is essentially "the proclamation of this Word of God *to man in his unbelief*," whether he is in the church or out of it.[21] Teaching, on the other hand, addresses itself primarily to those in the church (although it may also be an effective approach to those outside) ; it is the function of the church established by God "that his work of grace may take place, not just at one decisive moment in a man's life, but throughout the whole of it."[22] Directed toward "claiming the whole of life for God,"[23] teaching is, like preaching, "the service of the Word of God."[24]

The Church and Christian Education

It has already been indicated in considering the doctrine of the Trinity that God's revelation of himself necessitated the creation of the church. Smart's treatment of the doctrine of the church is too extensive to be covered here, but it is important to note the relationship of the church to the Word, the importance of church history, and the purpose of the church.

The church is called into being by the Word and exists in the service of the Word. Apart from revelation, it does not really exist. If the church fails in its ministry, "the Word of God is able to call into being another Church for its service. It has happened more than once."[25] This says decisively that "the Word creates the Church, not the Church the Word," although the two "belong together."[26]

One important function of Christian education, therefore, is to remind the church of its history, for it is the story of God's carrying forward of his purpose. This includes not only biblical history but church history, for the history of the church is really a commentary on the Bible, an interpretation in life and thought of what man has found there. No church and no believer can exist "on the pin point of the present moment."[27] There must always be reference to the past, to the church's "memory of itself . . . the dimension of depth in its existence."[28] Thus there is an obligation to teach history in such a way that a believer may know himself to be a part of "the Church of the ages."

Something of the purpose of the church has already been suggested. Its destiny is "to be the human instrumentality through which God will carry forward the redemptive purpose that he has revealed in Jesus Christ."[29] Smart has a strong emphasis on the church as "the body of Christ and the servant of the Word,"[30] an emphasis which seems to point more toward the *mission* of the church than toward the individual benefits members derive from its fellowship. There is certainly no overlooking of the importance of fellowship, but fellowship is one of the "fruits of faith." The "community of faith" has its "common center in God," and "their openness toward God calls for a corresponding openness toward each other."[31] The emphasis is on man's response to God's revelation, not on what happens to him through fellowship. In his participation in the purpose of the church, his giving himself to that which is outside himself, he receives salvation and achieves his destiny.

It would seem logical to conclude that the efforts of Christian educators would be directed less toward building "redemptive fellowship" than toward "training *to be* the Church in the world of today."[32]

The Purpose of Christian Education

Almost anything that could be said about the purpose of Christian education has already been suggested, but it is possible to summarize in terms of *discipleship*.

> Our goal must be no lesser goal than that which Jesus and the apostles had before them. We teach so that through our teaching God may work in the hearts of those whom we teach to make of them disciples wholly committed to his gospel, with an understanding of it, and with a personal faith that will enable them to bear convincing witness to it in word and action in the midst of an unbelieving world.[33]

This is more than character education. It recognizes the centrality of the church as the sphere within which Christian education takes place—the church which, though a human and limited channel of communication, is God's appointed instrument through which he continues to work for the redemption of the world. If Christian education is to be the "servant of revelation," it works with the hope that, by God's grace, children, youth, and adults may "find their life's fulfillment in being members of the very body of Christ and sharers in his mission."[34]

Revelation and the Process of Christian Education

Revelation is a dynamic, ongoing process in which the living Lord of history continues to reveal himself by what he does and to establish a relationship with man within which he makes redemption possible. Such is the view of Randolph Crump Miller. God's "mighty acts" in the history of Israel and the early church together with the interpretation of the meaning of those acts constitute the biblical revelation. When men see that "all of life is the creation of God,"[35] and begin interpreting experiences of their own individual and corporate lives in the light of the biblical revelation, they see that God is still acting, drawing them to himself and to wholeness of personality with "persuasive grace."

Christian education, then, becomes the process of moving along with God's continuing revelation. It involves starting with the Christian truth, formulated in theological terms as the "truth-about-God-in-relation-to-man,"[36] and helping persons comprehend the relevance of that truth for every aspect of life as it is interpreted from within the living reality of a relationship with God and with other persons through him. When Christian education actually becomes the process of helping truth to be experienced and interpreted, it demonstrates the true relevance of the Christian revelation and overcomes many false dichotomies of the past in its recognition of the "organic relation between doctrine and experience, between content and method, between truth and life."[37] The comprehensiveness of this view, with its drive toward seeing unity and continuity in experience and in God's revelatory acts, necessitates further consideration of the meaning of revelation, of its relationship to theology, and of its implications for the purpose of Christian education.

Event and Interpretation

Miller says that for Christian education "the view of revelation with its theory of knowledge and truth will determine the kind of authority used, the emphasis on content, the choice of methods, and the desired ends."[38] His whole philosophy of Christian education is a demonstration of this fact. Although he uses the words "relationship," "relevance," and "theology" more frequently than the word "revelation," these other concepts acquire their full significance only against an understanding of God's revelation as encompassing all creation and all history. Such a statement leads to the expectation that Miller's views on revelation will display an affinity with Temple's, and that is indeed the case. Agreement with Temple will be obvious as particular interpretations of Miller's "theory of knowledge and truth" are considered.

What is truth and how is it to be known? "Truth as we know it arises from our interpretation of events of experience."[39] Perhaps it might be said that the essence of truth is in the experienced events, and the formulated truth is in the interpretation of events. The phrase "as we know it" is important as indicating that truth becomes such for any person only within his own experience; that is the way truth is "known." Or it may be said that "truth may be acquired only through the interpretation of experience."[40] "Revelation," then, is "that particular segment of truth that arises from the interpretation of our relationships with God."[41]

This statement does not indicate a limitation of God's activity to one segment of experience, for he is Lord of all of life; it means that whenever a person becomes conscious of God's hand in any experience and thereby is made aware of his relationship to God, revelation occurs. Moreover, this statement points both to the fact that "the source of all truth and hope is God himself, revealed to us by his mighty acts in history," and that this "continuing" revelation would not occur were it not for the possibility of approaching experience with the Christian "given" of a point of view from which interpretation would be made.[42] All these considerations raise the question of general and special revelation, and of the role of reason and experience in revelation.

Although Miller does not engage in any polemic about general and special revelation, his assumption is clearly that the universe becomes intelligible only in terms of God's revelation in it. Man's faith "that a personal God stands behind the universe gives it a meaning that cannot result from the findings of science."[43] God stands behind the universe as creator and acts through its laws dependably. If God is creator, "there is much truth about him that may come to any mind that is open and alert."[44] There is, then, a general revelation. But there is also "a specific revelation in Christ which is the culmination of the acts of God in history as recorded in the Old Testament and as kept alive for us in the traditions of the Church."[45] Therefore it may be said that "within the Bible is the unique, final, and saving revelation of God."[46] There is no distinction between natural and revealed religion. Specific revelation, for Miller, becomes the perspective for interpretation of God's working everywhere.

God is constantly at work within his covenant relationship with his people to mold them into his servants and to speak to other men through them.[47] As Lord of history, God works through the church, social action, individuals, or other channels, "revealing himself supremely in the Bible and subordinately in every function of nature." This "orderly" way of God's working Miller sees as a contrast to the "sovereign piece-meal fashion" of revelation as presented by Barth and Kierkegaard. They both miss the point that "there is a continuity to revelation, and reason is the means whereby we grasp its meaning."[48]

This recognition of the interrelatedness of reason and experience with both general and special revelation is made though an approach which Miller calls an "enriched empiricism."[49] Not only those beliefs which arise "from our common human experiences," but also those which have their source in tradition, the

Bible, and non-religious knowledge may be tested by "the method of observation, experimental behavior, and rational inference."[50] This does not mean that the Christian faith rests upon any method. It rests upon God, who "is always in experience, and . . . always beyond experience."[51] One is thus forced to go "*beyond* empiricism.*" The fact that God is present and acting, combined with the assumption that "God *is* what he *does*," means that one comes to know him better through experience.[52] Even the doctrine of the Trinity "is a fundamentally sound and enduring attempt to translate the richness of men's experience of God into abstract terms."[53]

Most of these statements relating to experience are taken from Miller's earlier writings, during a time when he said specifically that the method he followed was that of empiricism. Although today there is a definite continuity with this position, terminology and emphases have changed somewhat. The crucial importance of personal relationships, as seen in Buber, Brunner, Farmer, and Howe, is increasingly recognized by Miller, but in such a way that more recent insights are related to the earlier emphasis on experience. For example, after quoting Temple's statement that "revelation is received in a living experience," and that "doctrines are inferences drawn from that revelation in the context provided by the rest of experience," Miller goes on to add that the value in these "doctrines" is in the "help they give in recovering the *relationships* so described," as though to equate experience and relationships.[54] There is a consistency in this building of "relationships" into the background of "experience," for a relationship is a particular kind of experience, and evidently Miller is saying that it is *here* revelation is most likely to occur and to be verified or communicated.

Wherever God is the center of personal relationships, those relationships may become the occasion for the experience of a faith-response to the prior grace of God. This is no less than a response to revelation along a broad front, with no restrictions on God's channels of mediation. Such a view is to be understood in distinction from Smart's, but, like Smart's, with everything as seen from the perspective of God's special revelation in Jesus Christ and in the Bible. This interpretation of Miller's position would place him within a viewpoint for which he expresses admiration.

> There is a reconstructed liberalism in American Christianity which points to the future of the Church with great hope. This liberalism is remarkably sane in its holding of a "central tradition" which is open to new interpretations of truth without discarding what is valuable in the old.[55]

In the field of philosophy of Christian education, such an interpretation would point to Miller as probably the leading representative today of the continuing liberal tradition—although the word "reconstructed" is important, for he rejects a "dated liberal doctrine" and tries to take into account such criticisms as those in Shelton Smith's *Faith and Nurture* through his constructive reformulation in a theological approach to Christian education.[56]

Continuing Revelation

Two points already touched upon need to be emphasized because of the important place they occupy in Miller's thinking. Revelation, because it is the action of the living God, continues, and *"the meaning of life is found in the living God, not in an idea."*[57] And this "meaning of life" becomes apparent primarily within the community of the church.

When revelation is viewed dynamically as an ongoing process, "the important fact for religious living is that the creative process itself is a continuing one and is the work of God *now*."[58] So long as the "living Christ is part of our everyday environment," the "door of revelation is not closed," although the revelation which has taken place in Christ and in his impact on history settles once and for all "the direction of revelation."[59] Wherever and however man responds freely to God's grace, "this is a revelation."[60]

"This revelation is normally found through participation in the shared life of the Christian community."[61] Such a statement can be made both because of the relationships that exist within the church, and because of the nature of the church. It is a theological insight to recognize that ordinarily God does not enter into personal relationship with anyone except through other persons. In this Miller agrees with Farmer. He develops this idea, drawing on both Buber and Howe.

> When a man works through such relationships, he treats each other person as a "Thou" and therefore discovers the "eternal Thou" behind each person. The "new structure of personal relationship," which is the church, provides the environment in which God's power of salvation is appropriated through faith.[62]

The area of revelation is therefore also the area of appropriation. It may even be said that the two are interdependent.

The church, as a "new structure of personal relationship," is the "redemptive and sustaining community of mankind, at least in its ideal formulation."[63] The "redemptive and sustaining" function of the church is Miller's emphasis, as over against Smart's view. Yet, just as Smart does not neglect the "fellowship" element, so Miller does not neglect seeing the church "in its highly exalted terms as the Body of Christ or the extension of the Incarnation or as God's agent of redemption."[64] The final question, he says, is not "What can the Church do for me?" but "What can I do for the Church?"[65] A follower of Christ is one "who is willing to lose his life in the service of his fellow men."[66]

Revelation and Theology

In his *Guide for Church School Teachers*[67] and in his analysis of "Christian Education Today,"[68] Miller points out the need for proceeding from a theological basis. Aware of criticisms of Christian education and believing that the "clue" to Christian education is "the rediscovery of a relevant theology,"[69] Miller set forth the kind of approach which has already been introduced. But is this emphasis on theology consistent with the early quoted statement about the determinative influence of the view of revelation? And how does this relate to Miller's approach to Christian education by way of biblical theology?

When it is recalled that revelation consists of the "coincidence of event and appreciation," then it becomes apparent that there is no conflict. Theology, defined for purposes of Christian education as "the truth-about-God-in-relation-to-man," might be considered the interpreted part of revelation. Biblical theology, then, would be the interpretation of God's action in Israel and the early church, recorded in the Bible and constituting the background for theological formulations in general. In turn, theology leads back to revelation through experience, for the kind of theology about which Miller speaks is a "relevant" theology. It stands in the background to give direction to developments, and in addition, perhaps more important, it represents the truth which can be so translated into life that it can be experienced there, primarily through relationships. That experience, reinterpreted against the theological background which gave it meaning, becomes revelatory, and leads back to building further content into the theology.

If theology is assigned this important role, the question arises as to whether one can arrive at and be sure of a "correct" theology. That is not Miller's chief concern, however. Believing that the fundamental center which makes religion or education Christian is "a personal relationship between the believer and the God of Jesus Christ," Miller does not require that one subscribe to particular theological tenets.[70] He chooses not to be dogmatic about the particular truth underlying curriculum, because the task of Christian education is not to teach theology as such.[71] It is to translate theology back into the truth it represents, where it can be learned in life and relationships. Again, here is a difference from Smart, who assigns to theology almost the task of heresy hunting, and who, it seems, thinks more in terms of correct words and creeds. The two men agree in seeing Christian education as a theological discipline. But the role theology plays in Christian education differs for them.

The Purpose of Christian Education

The intent in revelation and in the biblical record is in agreement with the purpose of Christian education, so that it might be said, in general terms, that "education is for redemption"—a redemption that occurs *now,* through "a revelation received by a community and communicated through community life."[72]

More specifically, Miller offers this statement:

> *The purpose of Christian education is to place God at the center and to bring the individual into the right relationship with God and his fellows within the perspective of the fundamental Christian truths about all of life.*[73]

The "perspective of the fundamental Christian truths about all of life" might be said to be "the framework of the revelation of God in Christ."[74] Accepting Christ, a person moves "toward that integration of personality that is the goal of religious education."[75] Integration, wholeness of personality, is not a goal *outside* of Christian education, to be achieved by various "means." It inheres in the *process* of Christian education, in the redemptive outreach of God's grace through which he seeks to bring all his children into relationship with himself.

Revelation and Its Corollary, Christian Education

That which distinguishes the Christian community from other communities, as Lewis J. Sherrill sees it, is that in it "the fact of revelation faces us."[76] Because of this, "all the offices of the church, from worship to administration, will be affected by the fact of revelation, and will derive their own distinctive nature and their own distinctive manner of functioning from it."[77] Revelation does not determine what education is; it only determines what *Christian* education is. That is to say, education exists within its own right, and there is room for all possible insights from educational philosophy and from sociological and psychological disciplines. But when education comes into relationship with revelation, although it has arisen out of a complex background of social, philosophical, and psychological factors, it takes on the "particular form" in which, as the corollary of revelation, it can best "participate in the total ministry of the Christian community to the total self of man."[78] What happens is that there develops a kind of dialogue between the doctrine of revelation and the theory of Christian education in which there is the possibility of mutual influence.

Sherrill's philosophy is developed from a concept of revelation as God's confrontation of man within an encounter in which there is a disclosure correlating with the predicament of man. He takes into account the media of revelation, and the context of the Christian community in which revelation is received. Each of these three subjects will be considered in turn before a concluding look at the relation between Christian education and revelation.

Confrontation and Encounter

For Sherrill, there is the fact of revelation, the report of revelation, and the doctrine of revelation. A doctrine of revelation consists of propositions drawn up from a study of reports of revelation, and is a body of changing generalizations. The report of revelation (both in the living witness of the church and in the written records of the Bible) points to the fact of revelation, but is not itself that fact.

There are two key words in Sherrill's understanding of revelation: confrontation and encounter. Confrontation refers to the divine initiative and activity, and encounter to man's experience of being confronted. Essentially, then, revelation is confrontation and takes place within the encounter. "To express the concept of revelation as confrontation in one of the simplest ways possible would be to say that God as Self confronts man as a self, and has disclosed himself to man."[79] Such a view places the initiative with God. What is revealed is not information about God, but God himself. Yet as God and man face each other within the encounter there is always both a togetherness and a separateness. Man is drawn toward God, but not absorbed in him. Human capacities "are engaged in receiving what is communicated in revelation."[80]

What is the content of God's disclosure? God himself is the content. What he discloses is "some aspect of infinite, perfect Selfhood, being unveiled in some form of relationship with finite, imperfect selves."[81] These aspects of Selfhood are themes of revelation, and their "meaning" may be considered "a word from the Lord" to "those who are able to pereceive it."[82] It may be necessary to report this meaning in informational or descriptive terms, but the fact remains that revelation itself is what happens in the meeting between man and God. There is much that is reminiscent of Brunner at this point.

What is the purpose of this self-disclosure of God to man? Sherrill says that *"revelation is redemptive in nature."*[83] Using insights and methods of analysis similar to those of Paul Tillich, Sherrill endeavors to understand who man is and what his situation is in today's world. The conclusion is that the human self has come to live in a state of anxiety and alienation which threatens its very existence. But if man can be drawn into a relationship with God, into a "self-to-Self relationship of mutual self-giving,"[84] there is a possibility of overcoming alienation and anxiety. Such is the purpose of revelation.

> Within such an encounter the rift within man himself can be healed, so that in being reconciled with God he is reconciled with himself. In such a case a man has found himself in grasping Another who had already gone forth to meet him. He has not been overpowered; he has been empowered with the power to become what he is.[85]

Media of Revelation

Insofar as the "themes of revelation" are also the "themes of the Bible," the question must be asked whether the revelation of God can be known only through the Bible, as Smart contends and as might be expected with the emphasis on confrontation. But that is not Sherrill's view. The Bible is the written report of original revelation and the response to it, and of "the response to dependent or derived revelation, which some prefer to call illumination."[86] It thus is "the principal source from which the church's teaching is drawn."[87] It stands in a position of such close relation with the church that both must be seen as "witnesses to revelation" acting "in human life as instruments to kindle illumination. These two, the church and the Bible, interact upon one another, each being capable of throwing fresh illumination upon the other."[88]

Original revelation, as it occurred and as it is recorded in the Bible, employed various media. Sherrill sees in the Bible four chief media "through which God reveals himself to man, and where his disclosure of himself to man is perceived." They are physical nature, human nature, events in history, and Jesus Christ.[89]

As Sherrill interprets the way these media are employed in revelation, one sees something of the influence of Temple. Revelation occurs only as the *meaning* in events is perceived under divine guidance. Original revelatory events "can be reperceived with new and deeper meaning as time passes."[90] This points to an imperative of the Judaic-Christian faith: "Remember!"[91] The influence of Richard Niebuhr, evident at other points as well, is seen here; remembering and perceiving bring meaning into the present as well as the past, "for this is *our* history, and it brings meaning into *our* lives."[92] This is an "appropriation of revelation" and "makes the history of the people of God a continuum, gives that history a basal place in Christian education, and puts one's own personal history in the great context of the history of redemption."[93]

The special occasion by which all occasions are to be interpreted, as Niebuhr would say, Sherrill finds in Jesus Christ, where acts and words took on flesh as the living Word. This is the culmination of God's self-disclosure to man, "the revelatory event by which all other revelation must be oriented."[94] The emphasis on the revelation in Jesus Christ is found consistently in Sherrill's writings. Jesus Christ is both a medium for revelation and revelation itself. Through participating in his death and resurrection, through knowing oneself to be both judged and accepted, one comes to know "the love of God and the power of God as in no other way."[95]

Koinonia

The church, along with the Bible, is witness to and instrument of revelation. It witnesses verbally, in proclamation and teaching, through worship, and through what it is by nature and what it does through its life. In its educational function, therefore, the church "is called upon to draw persons into a Christian community which (a) bears witness to revelation and which (b) bears witness to the divine re-creation and redemption of life in the relationships between the members of that community."[96]

As Sherrill views the church, he sees not only an objective witness, but the place where revelation continues and is appropriated. God may confront man anytime, anywhere, but *"the normal scene of revelation is the scene where fellowship exists."*[97] The nature of the fellowship can best be described as *koinonia*, a communion, a sharing, a participating in that which binds together believers and God. The reason the *koinonia* is the scene of revelation is that in it God, as Spirit, is present and continues to reveal himself in redemptive disclosure received within and sustained by that same *koinonia*. It is not the experience of *koinonia* that is revelatory, but "what happens in the encounter between God as Self and man as a self."[98]

Recognizing the psychological significance of relationships, Sherrill has drawn especially upon Harry Stack Sullivan, Otto Rank, and Karen Horney. What he finds expressed theologically and psychologically, he also finds expressed biblically. Jesus himself placed first importance on "the realm of man's relationships," dealing "with the relationship between men first from the standpoint of man's relationship with God."[99] Perhaps that is why "the New Testament conception of redemption is kept within the area of relationships," and why, furthermore, "the idea of the church as the Body of Christ gives Christianity one of the most profound conceptions of society ever expressed. . . . a society within whose relationships the divine pledge of redemption from guilt is meant to be realized."[100]

Revelation and Christian Education

Throughout the history of Judaic-Christian education, Sherrill finds an interaction between religion and education. "The religion produces the education, the education then produces more of its own kind in religion, whether it is a case of institutional forms or of persons."[101] The particular form of the interaction which has been under discussion is that between the doctrine of revelation and education. It is the responsibility of the theologian "to elucidate the nature and import of revelation," and the responsibility of the educator to acquaint himself with that doctrine and "inquire what the implications are for Christian education."[102] Perhaps it might be said that while the *process* of Christian education and the *fact* of revelation are to be seen in relationship to the perception and appropriation of revelation, it is the *doctrine* of revelation and the *theory* of education which determine implications of revelation for teaching and administering. Thus the relation of dialogue between the theologian and the educator.

When Christian education is understood as the corollary of revelation, then it becomes distinct from all other education. It is concerned with the total self and the changes that take place in the depths of the self responding to God. It is distinctive because of the nature of the society in which it is carried on, and because of the nature of the results for which it hopes. This coming to Christian education from within the Christian faith as a starting point leads to a recognition of "the unique nature of Christian education."[103]

> *Christian education is the attempt, ordinarily by members of the Christian community, to participate in and to guide the changes which take place in persons in their relationships with God, with the church, with other persons, with the physical world, and with oneself.*[104]

There is, then, a place for "human participation in bringing about the encounter between man and God."[105] Confrontation can exalt divine initiative in a way that stimulates human initiative and responsibility, as is done biblically through the doctrine of the covenant and of the *koinonia*. But as men participate with and influence one another in their responses to God, they must witness to the fact of revelation in such a way that revelation speaks for itself. Aims are therefore to be stated in such general terms as drawing men to "sustain the relationships and respon-

sibilities of life as children of God," or in other similar ways.[106]
Too specific a statement draws educators into "the business of
trying to predetermine for others what their behavior and what
their feelings should be,"[107] whereas in reality Christian education purposes more to prepare for the encounter which "leads
primarily not to knowledge *about* God, but to knowledge *of*
God." That is to say, it leads not to *gnosis* but to *epignosis*.[108]

Summary

Among the writers considered, the areas of consensus on the
implications for Christian education of the meaning of revelation probably would lie in recognition of these factors: (a) the
determinative influence of revelation for Christian education; (b)
the necessity for a theological and educational partnership in participation in the mission of the church; (c) the initiative and
continuing activity of God, with a lessened confidence in man's
ability to determine or control results through educational processes, although as educator he has deeper motivation to work than
formerly; (d) increased emphasis on the centrality of the Bible
for Christian education; and (e) the organic relationship between
education and the Christian community, in both church and
home.

At some of these points there are differences of interpretation.
For example, with Sherrill revelation is not a matter of a "content" which imposes itself upon and determines education by virtue of its intrinsic authority, as for Smart. Nor is it a matter of
permeating or determining Christian education from within, as
an inner principle, as for Miller. Rather, the doctrine of revelation and theory of education stand in dialogue with each other,
and revelation itself may transform the process of education. Or
again, the centrality of the Bible, for Smart, means that revelation
is confined to God's acts in Christian history as recorded there,
and therefore the Bible is the sole way to knowledge of God.
Miller, with his emphasis on experience and relationships, and

Sherrill, with his on *koinonia,* stand in contrast to Smart both in these emphases and in their unwillingness to assign to the Bible quite the exclusive role he assigns it in relation to revelation. Yet in all three positions, revelation is redemptive in purpose, and the reason for seeking an understanding of revelation is that Christian education may find its role in relation to that understanding and to that purpose.

It would seem evident that Miller carries on the Anglican tradition, exemplified by Temple. Smart represents the neo-Reformation tradition set forth in a particularly clear fashion by Barth. Sherrill, standing close to Brunner in his "encounter" concept of revelation, shows also the influence of Tillich and Richard Niebuhr. Yet there is no clear-cut or limited line of influence; all three educators are aware of and refer to emphases of all the theologians represented here. It is evident that these three representative Christian educators are sensitive to the theological climate of the times, endeavoring to develop the implications for the discipline they represent. Perhaps this is partly true because they come to the educational work from a theological background which in part explains their particular contributions. What about the position of other writers in the field?

A rather wide survey of writings in the field of Christian education indicates, as might be expected, that some writers, for all practical purposes, ignore both the fact and the doctrine of revelation. Others increasingly reflect a concern for and a use of the doctrine of revelation as more recently explicated, although no other persons have given such comprehensive consideration to the subject as Smart, Miller, and Sherrill. Some can be rather closely identified with the positions already described—Norman Langford and Elmer Homrighausen with Smart; Reuel Howe, a major representative of the "theology of relationships," with Miller; Charles Johnson with Sherrill.

Still other persons, like Mary Alice Jones and Howard Grimes, show themselves to be more in the tradition of Miller and Sherrill than of Smart. Two other persons at first impression seem to begin at a point closer to Smart, but actually this is not the case, and the positions they work out are independent, although reflecting the theological concerns of the time. Campbell Wyckoff, who sees "the gospel of God's redeeming activity in Jesus Christ"[109] as the guiding principle for the building of a theory of Christian education, is particularly concerned to relate educational theory to theology. Iris Cully,[110] concerned to communicate the good news of Jesus Christ in such a dynamic way that it will come alive continually, recognizes revelation to be confrontation, but neither she nor Wyckoff builds theory primarily from a point of view of revelation.

Another writer, Paul H. Vieth, represents something of a synthesis of the three positions described here as he continues along the line of thought set forth in *The Church and Christian Education*, indicated as marking the beginning of the current developments in Christian education, particularly with respect to the doctrine of revelation and the use of the Bible. He would agree with Smart in seeing a "gospel-centered" Christian education, purposing to "confront and control persons by the Christian Gospel."[111] The goal is "discipleship."[112] He would see the chief "content" of Christian education as God. Yet Vieth believes that God reveals himself in many ways; he recognizes too keenly the role of experience and the determinative influence of relationships to be in entire agreement with Smart. Moreover, in seeing revelation and Christian education as corollaries he seems closer to Sherrill than to either Smart or Miller. His mediating influence becomes evident in his view that, whereas revelation is determinative of the purpose of the church's educational work, Christian education in its practical outworking is still an educational as well as a theological discipline.

That, in fact, seems to be the direction of thought for both Wyckoff and Cully. However that may be, it seems safe to conclude that much of the new vitality in Christian education has come from a concern for the meaning of revelation, and to predict that the doctrine of revelation will continue to be a determinative factor in the development of philosophy of Christian education.

IV The Nature of the Biblical Witness

Christian educators of the earlier part of this century, criticized both for ignoring the results of higher criticism and for their unquestioned acceptance of those results, were faced with a dilemma. The great majority of people, fearful of the undermining of the authority of the Bible by historical research, often forced educators into a compromise in their interpretation. On the other hand, the interpretation which resulted from recognition of research came to be an account of the origins and development of Christianity without full attention to the real meaning in biblical history. Both biblical scholars and educators have thus been faced with the need to relate historical criticism and theological interpretation.

Beyond that, as educators engage in the effort to interpret the nature of the biblical witness in relationship to the teaching of the Bible, they are forced to deal directly with some basic questions. Is the Bible the Word of God or a "resource" for Christian living? What is its message and how is it formulated? What does this mean for Christian education? Views of James Smart, Randolph Crump Miller, and Lewis J. Sherrill, considered in the preceding chapter, are presented here in the order named as they answer these questions in the light of their understanding of revelation and on the basis of the work of biblical scholars and theologians.

The Word of God

The essence and totality of the biblical witness is that God, sovereign Lord of the universe and of history, has spoken and continues to speak through the Scriptures. Such is James Smart's position. This speaking is a self-revelation which is not truth in general, but *"the* Truth, which is the redemption and the reconciliation of the whole of life to God."[1] Because "in the order of faith, revelation is always first and all else issues from it,"[2] the biblical record witnesses to and is a channel for revelation, derives its authority from that to which it witnesses, is to be interpreted as the living Word, and occupies a central place in the curriculum of Christian education.

The Record and the Word

The Bible may be called the Word of God, Smart says, but only because "in the Scriptures there comes to us a revelation of God which does not come in any other way."[3] The Scriptures and revelation are not identical; the infallibility of the Bible rests in its message, not in its words. Thus it must not be forgotten that the Bible is a record employing human words as means of communication. It is also more than a record. It is "the field of revelation."[4] Two important points follow. The Bible is *the* "field of revelation," not one among many, and it is such because God continues to reveal himself through it. He does not preserve abstract truths or information about himself in lifeless words.

This is not to say that revelation is bound between the covers of a book; indeed, "it fills all creation and has to do with every detail of human life, for all things are of God."[5] However, it is not "all creation" that *leads* to knowledge of God. Nature and conscience are not reliable sources of truth. The one such source is the "record preserved by the Church of how God revealed himself to it and so called it into being" and is to be received within that community created by the Word if God is to reveal himself anew.[6] Smart summarizes his conviction that the Bible and its message are unique, saying that "God speaks to man through the Scriptures a word of judgment and mercy which, if it is not heard in this place, is not heard at all."[7] When the biblical message is heard, the knowledge which comes brings new life. Smart even speaks of a "Protestant doctrine of the Real Presence" in the Scriptures.[8] What man receives is not knowledge about God but a meeting with him through the Bible. Thus it may be said that through the Bible "the Word that was once heard and spoken sounds ever anew into the life of the world."[9]

Biblical Authority

What has already been said about "content" in relation to Smart's understanding of revelation is the key to his understanding of biblical authority. The fact that it is God who uses the Bible as a channel of revelation is the explanation of the Bible's authority. It is the reason Smart can say, "The Bible does not require our defenses of it or our apologies for it. It is quite able to take care of itself. Above all, what it needs is to be laid open before men with complete honesty that it may speak its own word in its own way."[10] When the Bible is allowed to speak for itself, it can assert its own authority. Man does not have to exercise "compulsion in matters of belief"; that is to trespass "upon God's prerogative." Man is "helpless to believe . . . until the truth evidences itself to him as the truth for him and makes that kind of claim upon him which it is impossible for him to escape."[11] Even this recognition of the inner testimony of the Spirit goes back, in the final analysis, to that which is the very basis of the Bible's authority. "There can be no compulsion except that which the truth contains in itself."[12]

This was the kind of authority the Bible exerted upon the Reformers. "The truth held them and possessed them so that they were no longer free."[13] Their loyalty to the Scriptures caused them to be driven out of the church "because they could not acknowledge the authority of an external Church to be superior to the authority of the truth of the Word of God."[14]

Here Smart touches upon a great ecumenical controversy, and again he sides with Barth. It has already been shown that Smart sees the church as having been created by the revelation which is the Word of God. However, it should be added that the *record* of revelation, the Bible, also is authoritative over the church, and is absolutely essential for its continuance. "It is the record of the Word of God that created the Church, and that is able to create the Church ever afresh when it is rightly heard and obeyed."[15] That is to say, in the Scriptures "the Church of Jesus Christ stands forth ever afresh in contrast to the Church as it is."[16] The constant call to that true church serves as a reforming power from within. It means that while people are called to discipleship within the church, it is not a call to conformity with the existing church accepted as ideal. The existing church must bring itself constantly under the authority of the Bible.

When all this is admitted, it must be added that Bible and church are inseparable. "God did not entrust his gospel to a book, but to a fellowship of disciples in whose hearts he writes his word and whom he empowers to be his witnesses by his indwelling spirit."[17]

Biblical Theology

The biblical witness, formulated as "message" or "gospel," is apprehended to be what it is from a theological perspective which presupposes God's speaking through the Bible and which assumes the kind of biblical authority just described. This raises the questions of the unity of the Bible, of principles of interpretation, and of the attitude toward biblical criticism.

That which gives the Bible its authority also gives it unity.

> The authority of the Scriptures is that there sounds forth from them a single Voice, completely consistent in its demands and its promises, manifesting from beginning to end one purpose and one will, and evidencing itself to the mind and heart and conscience of man as the voice of God.[18]

Because the witness of the Bible is to the one God, there is only one gospel. The view "that the Law is in the Old Testament and the Gospel is in the New, or that God is a God of justice in the Old Testament and a God of love in the New" is "unsatisfactory."[19] If law and gospel, judgment and mercy, belong together throughout the Bible and give evidence of their one source, so does God's covenant relationship with Israel witness to the one gospel of salvation. The creative power of God's revelation which made a band of unorganized slaves into the nation of Israel is

continuous with the redemptive power offered within the covenant relation of God with his people in the church. All of this
means that there can be no real disjunction between the Old and
New Testaments. The Bible witnesses to one Word incarnate in
Jesus Christ.

This view of the unity of the Bible is evidence of the fact that
historical events have been interpreted theologically, from the
perspective of God's revelation in Jesus Christ as normative.
Smart holds that all Bible study, if it is to be effective, must be
carried on with this kind of interpretation. He has not worked
out detailed principles of interpretation, but he is consistent in
interpreting the Bible as the Word of God, and he takes his position with those biblical scholars who encourage the trend toward
biblical theology.

In general, he seems to place more emphasis on unity than on
diversity within the Bible, more on the interpretation of God's
action than on historical details. Rejecting both a single-minded
devotion to the Bible as God's Word, which repudiates man's
right to use his intelligence in investigating Scripture, and a
single-minded devotion to scientific truth, which can find no room
in the Bible for a unique revelation of God, Smart sees the possibility of overcoming the false antithesis of the early twentieth
century. The current rediscovery of the Bible has brought with
it "the emergence of a Biblical scholarship that takes the Bible
in earnest as the revelation of God which it claims to be and
which the Church has consistently recognized that it is."[20]

The question about biblical criticism, then, has already been
answered. The "scientific approach to the Biblical records," when
it is found "in combination with an earnestness about the Bible
as the revelation of God," is at all times to be encouraged.[21] What
does this mean for Christian education? It condemns what has
been "the most characteristic feature of the church school's han-
dling of the Bible"—timidity.[22] To regain the respect of intelligent people, the teaching of the Bible must be characterized "by
a thoroughgoing openness and honesty in every detail of interpretation." When men come to understand the essential nature

of the Bible and of its authority, their minds will be liberated to "roam through the Bible with a new freedom."[23] It is therefore the responsibility of Christian educators to remedy in the present the grievous past error of dealing apologetically or fearfully with critical questions. Moreover, it is to be recalled that it is "faith in God that saves, and not the particular viewpoint we may hold on this or that matter in Scripture."[24] That is why a theological interpretation calling one's attention to the meaning in events is of such basic importance.

Christian Education and the Centrality of the Bible

If the Bible brings the gospel to men, and if the nature of the witness is such that God's word of judgment and mercy is heard there or nowhere at all, then no justification is needed for making the Bible central in Christian education. Its role in Christian education corresponds to the centrality of the Bible for the life of the church as a whole. It is central in the church in that education in the Scriptures is education into the church, the body of Jesus Christ. It is central in the curriculum in that the purpose inherent in the Bible is the purpose of Christian education.

In relation to the church, study of the Bible leads to a right knowledge of what the church is, and is the means for "the growth of persons into the existing Church."[25] But an educational program centered around the Bible may even make men "rebels" within the church, working for its reform, as it builds a revolutionary force, a reforming power, reaching out from within toward the true church of Jesus Christ.

In relation to curriculum, teaching the Bible is never to be identified with "the transmitting of information about the Bible and its contents."[26] This would not lead people to become witnessing disciples. Nor does teaching the Bible exclude reference to life situations. The Bible unrelated to life cannot be the word of God. Therefore the Scriptures "must not be studied *by themselves alone* and divorced from the life situations of today in which the revelation of God must take place."[27] When people, through the Bible, are brought "into living fellowship with the prophets and apostles and with Jesus Christ himself," then the word of God comes alive and has "its cutting edge in these Christians of today."[28] This is the reason for the unique place of the Bible.

The Drama of Redemption

The term "drama of redemption" is the most concise way to designate Randolph Crump Miller's understanding of the nature of the biblical witness. It shows the connection between his concept of revelation and his understanding of the Bible. Revelation is God's action in history plus the interpretation of the meaning in that action; the Bible records the events and gives the interpretation of men who observed themselves to be the beneficiaries of God's gracious action. God takes the initiative in revelation; he is the "chief actor" in the biblical drama. Moreover, the term points to the content and structure of the Bible, to be considered here in relation to God's mighty acts seen as drama, and to God's purpose of redemption proclaimed through the biblical message of "good news." This consideration will contribute to an understanding of Miller's use of "drama" and will necessitate raising the question of the authority of this drama and of ways in which it may be interpreted for purposes of Christian education.

The Mighty Acts of God

The Bible may be considered a record of "God's mighty acts in history." Through the record God's revelation is seen as an unfolding drama of redemption. Such a view is a contrast to an earlier view in which it was primarily the record of man's search for God. God is seen as the one who takes the initiative, working to bring man into relationship with himself and with his fellow men. But the Bible is also an account of "man's response to God's grace," so that it is "man's history as well as God's."[29] It is an account of man's understanding of God and who he is. In that sense, the Bible is "a progressive revelation in terms of what man has learned, although we believe that God does not change."[30] Nevertheless, whatever man sees and says about God, it is always from the perspective of a relationship with God.

In the "mighty acts" approach to the Bible, Miller agrees with G. Ernest Wright, drawing from time to time upon his *God Who Acts: Biblical Theology as Recital*. Both men see the specific Jewish history set within the context of all history, and holding for all history the hope of redemption. For Miller, emphasis on God's mighty acts *in history* points up the fact that "Christianity is primarily an historical rather than a metaphysical religion." This means that "the center of the approach to God will be through Jesus Christ, and Jesus will always be seen against the historical background of the Incarnation."[31]

There is a particular value in approaching the Bible through study of the events it recounts. This is a way of "getting beneath the differences,"[32] for whether liberals or conservatives are doing the studying, they "have to deal with the same events."[33] Yet these events must always be interpreted, if they are to have meaning; therein lies biblical theology. There will be differences in details of interpretation, but the generalized view of the Bible as a "drama of God's mighty acts in history" offers possibilities for a framework of agreement.[34]

The formulation of the biblical message in terms of drama will remind one of Bernhard Anderson's approach. Miller's analysis in terms of five acts in the drama differs somewhat from Anderson's three acts with subdivisions in scenes, and was worked out independently.[35] The five acts in the biblical drama are these: Creation; Covenant; Christ; Church; Consummation. In each of them God is at work, "eternally creative, continually acting, and seeking to bring men into the right relationship with him."[36]

The Message and Purpose of the Drama

The message is "God's good news," proclaimed in the Bible from beginning to end in the story of God's mighty acts. It is "the story of God's grace and man's hope." The "good news" is the offer of salvation. The hope is for a restored relationship with God, for integration of personality, for fullness of life.[37] The purpose of the drama is not simply to tell a story, then, but to draw men to become participants in it, and thus to experience the reality of the redemption God offers through his acts.

Authority and Freedom

The Bible is "the basic source book of Christian theology," Miller says, and the record of God's revelatory acts.[38] Those revelatory acts, "culminating in the historical events of the life, and death, and resurrection of Jesus Christ, which are summarized in the doctrines of the Incarnation and Atonement," can be learned about only through the Bible.[39] Accordingly, "the indisputable claim made by all Protestant Christians" is this: *"Within the Bible is to be found a unique, true, final, and saving revelation of the one true God."*[40] Therefore the Bible, which contains "all things necessary for salvation," is "our basic authority."[41]

These statements concerning the authority of the Bible are in general terms, and need supplementing by answers to three questions: What is the nature of the authority exerted by the Bible? What is its relation to other authorities? How does it become effective in the life of the individual Christian? A summary of answers for the first two questions is to be found in *The Clue to Christian Education*.

> It is the thesis of this book that the source of all authority and all freedom is God, who has revealed himself to men in events of history and in nature. The primary seat of revelation and thus of authority is found in the Bible as interpreted by the concept of "the mind of Christ." All other authorities, such as the Church, the creeds, the ministry or the episcopate, reason, and conscience, are inferior to the authority of Holy Scripture.[42]

This points out specifically the fact stressed especially by Barth, Richard Niebuhr, and Smart, that authority rests in *God,* not in infallible words of a book. Miller's particular emphasis is the necessity of understanding authority in relation to freedom. "Only when authority is correlated with freedom, when authority is self-validating because its truth can be demonstrated, when

the Bible and traditions and creeds portray and reveal the living
God in Christ, is there Christian authority."[43]

Why is freedom so essential? Basically, the answer is that persons have been granted powers of judgment and decision. Within
these powers lies the right to choose the authority to which they
will submit. Having made the decision for Jesus Christ, the
Christian finds a second level of authority *within* the authority
he has chosen, and comes to know that "both freedom and authority are subsumed under the concept of loyalty to the living
God and to the Christian community."[44] Both the "minimum
freedom" and the freedom within authority necessitate an act of
the will which prevents the imposition of any kind of "arbitrary
or external authority." Religious authority "is not coercive power,
but rather partakes of the nature of moral persuasion, which is
both trustworthy and living in its hold upon men who admit
such authority."[45] Because this authority "operates through the
sense of obligation," it "presupposes freedom as basic to its existence."[46]

It has been indicated that the Bible's authority is basic, or primary, but the suggestion is that it has a relation to other authorities. Creeds have a "derivative authority only." They are summary statements of faith or belief in God, and find their validity
in Scripture.[47] Interpretations by the ministry are always in
"terms of submission to the authority of Scripture itself."[48] The
same thing is true of the church, although it is important to remember that the church must make decisions in controversies
of faith, and that the "corporate nature of the Church's judg-
ments under God makes its authority superior to that of the individual."[49] Besides this, the church brings to bear upon the
Scriptures the understanding of history, reason, and the experience of the race, particularly "of those who have shared the
Christian revelation."[50] The Bible, therefore, can never be a sur-
rogate for the church.

Furthermore, the church has a role to play in making the authority of the Bible effective in the life of the individual. Unless
the church can exhibit "that quality of life which the New Tes-

tament reveals," the Bible cannot be "taught."[51] And unless individuals experience the truth of the gospel for themselves, all authority will remain external, and beliefs will not become faith personally appropriated. In summary, then, it can be said that "authority and freedom are blended together in the worshipping community which has its roots in an historical revelation."[52]

The Mighty Acts Interpreted

Events must be interpreted if they are to have significance. But before they can be interpreted, there must be a point of view from which interpretation begins. That point, for Miller, is "the mind of Christ." It provides "a perspective in terms of basic attitudes by which the remainder of the Bible can be understood," and has the advantage of combining all possible objective knowledge from the Synoptics with insights provided by history and the individual's "free choice."[53] Events interpreted from this perspective result in a biblical theology which is historical and theological at the same time. This is Miller's way of bringing together biblical scholarship and theology, as he is able to do by placing the whole Bible within the framework of drama.

Two things must be said about this framework. One is that "this framework is no arbitrary device; it comes from seeing the theological implications of Biblical history as the events are clarified through adequate scholarship."[54] A second point is that the framework "comes from seeing ourselves as living within Act IV (Church) of the drama of redemption, within the community of the Spirit whose book is the Bible."[55] Caught up in the drama which continues God's outreach to man, the church can understand the Bible "because it is addressed to the Church out of which it came."[56]

The gap that exists between scholars and laymen must be overcome by giving accurate information about biblical research and by helping people see that biblical criticism does not "threaten" but rather can "clarify" their faith.[57] In addition, there is a need for encouraging Bible study in line with the interpretation suggested here, along with the detailed help found in the "Principles of Interpretation" from the World Council of Churches. When this happens, then the fragmented, timid approach to the Bible will be replaced by an acceptance of biblical scholarship which will be helpful in correcting errors, and will enable people to "see the Bible as a whole, against its historical background, with the people portrayed as the Bible portrays them."[58]

Seeing the Bible as a whole is possible when it is viewed as drama, and when God's redemptive purpose runs through all the events of both Old and New Testaments. This is Miller's approach to unity in the Bible—through drama and not through relating the Testaments as law and gospel, or through a typology that finds Jesus Christ in all Old Testament events, or through a Calvinistic unity of revelation. The parts of the drama can be understood only when the whole drama is seen.

The power experienced by God's people in the Bible, in their response to him, is available to men today if they are confronted by the gospel revealed in the Bible. This cannot be done by words only. The task of Christian education is "to look at the Bible and see how it can become a means of redeeming and sustaining grace to all God's creatures."[59] The drama of redemption must be interpreted and related to the experience of all ages if the Bible is to fulfill this role. What this does is to point to the problem of the relevance of the Bible, for it is as the biblical witness is made relevant that its purpose is achieved and persons are brought into a "believing and saving relationship with the living Christ as revealed in the Bible story."[60]

The Gospel of God

Man, who is "his own lost continent," as Lewis J. Sherrill says, finds within himself a rift so deep he cannot escape the recognition that "to be human is to be exposed to tragedy such as no subhuman creature could ever know."[61] The fact that "this tragedy can be overcome and surmounted is the central theme in revelation."[62] It is a fact proclaimed as the core of the biblical message, in its witness to revelation—the fact of the good news that the Kingdom of God is at hand, and within that Kingdom salvation is to be found. This good news is the Christian gospel. It is a salvation offered through God's continuing confrontation of man in judgment and mercy, formulated in the Bible in terms of themes corresponding to the human predicament. But the Bible is more than a verbalized hope or an objective statement of themes. Within the life of the church it becomes a channel for encounter between man and God, holding out to man the power to respond to God's love and thus to become the self which is his destiny.

The Gospel and the Kingdom

The profound note of pessimism sounded by Sherrill in his analysis of the human situation leads on to the query whether there is any hope at all for man. It is to that question that the Bible speaks. The answer is the message contained in the Bible that "God's love is stronger than man's anxiety, and can overcome it."[63] Both the facts of Jesus' ministry and the content of his preaching and teaching demonstrate the deliverance that he offers and brings. Sherrill's analysis of the first three Gospels "makes it clear that the 'preaching' of Jesus was not the rather omnibus activity which is now often designated by that term."

> It had a specific content, called the "Gospel." This "Gospel" was the Good News that the Kingdom of God is here, at hand. That was an indirect way of proclaiming that at long last the awaited Deliverer, the Christ, had come.[64]

When one moves from the proclamation of the gospel to the ministry of Jesus, "it is plain that He counted no human ill of any sort, whether physical, nervous, mental, social, economic, or political, as being beyond the range of the gospel's power to invade and conquer. *How* this might be so then became the subject of His teaching."[65] And as to the teaching, Sherrill says that "if there is one theme that runs through all the recorded teaching of Jesus, that theme is the Kingdom of God."[66]

What is the Kingdom of God, in which all of Jesus' ministry

of preaching, teaching, and healing seems to coalesce? Consider the matter first negatively. The Kingdom is not "a program of social reform" derived from Jesus' teachings, nor "a symbol for an ideal social order." Moreover, "just as the Kingdom of God, as described in the Gospels, gives us no blueprint for remaking the present, so also it does not offer us the statistical and factual data of history before the events have taken place."[67] Prediction of the future is in highly symbolical terms, pointing with confidence to God's ultimate triumph. It allows for no listing of signs indicative of a visitation from heaven bringing with it an external redemption. Nor can man himself achieve this external redemption through "tinkering with the environment." No more can he heal himself by the "religious busyness" which is an effort to escape meeting God and being transformed by him.[68]

Positively, the Kingdom of God refers to "that sovereignty of God over the individual in a personal relation."[69] The Kingdom becomes a reality when the relationship of love replaces the malignant relationship with God which is the "bottom of a man's hell."[70] The radical cure reaching to the root of the malignant relationship is offered by God through Jesus Christ, in Christ's "going down into the abyss of death with and for his beloved," and in the Resurrection, standing "both as example and as pledge of a spiritual power able to shatter the determinisms of life and even the determinism of death itself."[71] The whole stream of Judaic-Christian history points to and illustrates this love of God which releases man from bondage and calls into being a new self. "The Gospel is proclaiming that these things are a fact, not a theory. They do not confront us for discussion, but for response."[72]

Thus it is to be noted that the biblical teaching portrays the Kingdom of God not only as promise, but also as claim. It is the claim of God the Lord, and the Kingdom is that which places "the major accent upon *God*" and which in the last analysis means total *"sovereignty of God over the individual."*[73] The biblical message is an affirmation of salvation offered within the Kingdom of God. The biblical witness to the hope in the Christian gospel calls men to respond in love, obedience, and a loyalty that transcends all other loyalties and becomes a "standard of reference by which all other claims of every kind may be tested."[74] When God's sovereignty is acknowledged in a faith response, which, "put in the simplest terms, is the outgoing of human love in response," it may be said that "a new self is being born or is at least struggling to be born 'of the Spirit.' "[75] Within this relationship with the sovereign Father-King, a person may enter into a new freedom within the Kingdom, a freedom made possible in no other way.

Themes of the Bible

> *Revelation is God's disclosure of himself in creation, in lordship, in vocation, in judgment, in redemption, in re-creation, in providence, and in the life of faith; the Bible contains these themes, and each of them is in correspondence with some profound human predicament.*[76]

It is the fact of confrontation which discloses to man both the nature of his predicament and the knowledge of some aspect of the selfhood of God which reveals to him the remedy. The biblical message, according to Sherrill's analysis of the Bible, is formulated in terms of these eight "themes." They are the clues to the relevance of the Bible and to the selection of materials for teaching purposes in the Christian community. They are not offered with the thought that they constitute a final list. As a matter of fact, what men perceive to be the themes of the Bible will change from time to time. The "doctrine of revelation changes in the church with the passing of time" and that affects the perception of themes in the Bible. The important thing is to select themes "with great attentiveness to what is in the Bible itself, so that they may be themes which spring out of the Bible and are not foisted upon it."[77]

Essentially it is Sherrill's understanding of revelation which lies behind his formulation of the biblical message in terms of themes, and which gives the principle of interpretation by which both the unity and diversity of that message may be ascertained. Themes are the *meaning* in historical events, and are what makes those events revelatory. Concrete, specific events of history are not to be identified with themes, but "when a long series of revelatory events speaks to one persisting human predicament, what is uttered in the long series of revelatory events becomes a theme."[78] A theme "hangs together," and speaks "in many ways to many men through centuries of time."[79]

Insofar as all these themes disclose something of God himself as he confronts man, and insofar as they persist through both Old and New Testaments, they may be said to be unifying factors in the biblical message. They do not appear in every book of the Bible, they are not sharply separated from one another, but they are "the notes on which the great symphony of redemption is constructed, and they keep on appearing and reappearing."[80] As these themes present the unity of the Bible, they also allow for its diversity. There will be tension between the parts of a theme as it appears in the Old and in the New Testament, or even in different parts of one Testament. Not all parts of a theme say the same thing, and each part must be allowed to "stand forth" in its own right "without being tampered with"; yet these parts are not "disparate fragments," but are organic to the "large purposeful movement of continuing Self-disclosure."[81]

The fact that "each of the themes comes to culmination in the life, death, and resurrection of Jesus Christ" means that the concept of the unity of the Bible rests ultimately in Jesus Christ.[82] Thus the principle by which the Bible is to be interpreted and the two Testaments related is the understanding of the nature of the revelation in Jesus Christ. Just as the early Christians reoriented themselves to the Old Testament in the light of their knowledge of Jesus Christ, so the church today must recognize the validity of the Jewish faith, but must perceive its meaning for the Christian community from the perspective of its fulfillment in Jesus Christ, who is himself the Word of God.

The Bible and the Church

Sherrill's assumption is that "the nature of the Bible should govern our purpose in using it";[83] he concludes that "the central purpose of using the Bible in Christian education is *to prepare the way for men to perceive God and respond to him in the present. We may call this the purpose of the continuing encounter.*"[84] This is a purpose consistent with the nature of the Bible and with the nature of the revelation to which it witnesses.

There are other purposes contributory to this central purpose, but always subsidiary to it. The function of remembrance of the religious community may be discharged by introducing members of the community to the revelatory events and persons which have gone into the making of the Jewish-Christian heritage. The themes of revelation, which always transcend all particulars of persons, places, or events, are nevertheless rooted in those particulars and can never be approached or understood apart from them. Here Sherrill is in agreement with both Barth and Niebuhr. Two other purposes, "of learning to think and communicate in terms of Biblical symbols," and "of inquiring whether the Bible throws any light upon the place where we stand at the present moment of existence,"[85] are also contributory to the central effort to prepare the way for the continuing encounter within the worshiping Christian community. Aside from the interaction between persons and the worship of the church, the Bible is lifeless.

What, then, is the nature of the authority of the Bible and what is its relation to the authority of the church? Sherrill does not deal systematically or in detail with these questions. His position seems to be that the Bible exerts over man a spiritual and a teaching authority, pointing to and mediating the power and wisdom of God. The authority comes to function as the church helps a person to become "involved" in the Bible rather than "put under pressure from the Bible."[86] Increasingly, as people come to "encounter the Bible itself and what it contains,"[87] they move toward the acceptance of that authority which is "the charter of liberty." This is a change of sovereignty which is "symbolically expressed in the act of publicly professing faith in Jesus Christ as Lord and Savior."[88]

> The change is from an external to an internal authority, and from a human to a divine authority. This does not necessar-

ily mean disavowing human authority, such as that of
parents, state, or church. But it knows a hierarchy of authority, wherein the authority of God is supreme.[89]

The divine authority which is mediated by the Bible is also
mediated by the church through a human authority "very responsive to the patterns and pressures that happen to prevail in
human society."[90] The church is not to be identified with the
Kingdom, the realm of the authority of God; the Kingdom transcends and stands over against the church, challenging the church
to overcome its splitness, to cast off its pretensions, and to avoid
the tyranny which arises when the church assumes it is identical
with the Kingdom. It is the role of the church "to be the scene
where man is confronted by the claims of the Kingdom of God,
that is, by God Himself."[91] And the primary source of man's
knowledge of God is the Bible, so that the Bible and the church
depend upon each other. But the two are also in tension because
the biblical revelation always keeps the church under the judgment of God. Moreover, the church, itself confronted by the
Bible, must so interpret the Bible that it does not usurp the
Bible's authority by standing between it and man with a doctrine
which dilutes or screens the biblical message. It is only as the
church constantly brings itself and its doctrines into the light of
the twofold form of the Word of God—the written word and the
living Word Jesus Christ—that it can become either "spokesman
for God" or the place above all others where there may occur
"this confronting of man by the living God who speaks through
His Word." This is at the "core of the church's business in the
world."[92]

This kind of authority is not dependent upon an infallible
book. It recognizes the human element in the Bible, so that, as
Sherrill says, "we need to use the Bible with due regard for all
the light that can be thrown upon it from historical, literary, or
textual criticism; or from research in archaeology, anthropology,
and psychology."[93] To do this puts man in a dilemma, however,
for "findings in all these fields of study are themselves subject to
error." Trying to escape from "the tyranny of an authoritarian

use of the Bible," man falls into "the equally authoritarian use of 'the latest results of scientific study,' which are then allowed to dictate what we may or may not do with the Bible."[94]

There are other temptations which beset the church and cause individual teachers to parade a "knowledge" which tends to "overwhelm the revelation of God."[95] But when "the core of the church's business in the world" and "the purpose of the continuing encounter" are recalled, then the Bible can more clearly speak its own message and bear its witness to revelation.

Summary

There seems to be a high degree of agreement among the writers considered at these points: (a) The Bible has a message, a gospel, which is God's word for man's redemption. That message is not to be identified with specific words of the Bible, but the words may become a channel of revelation as God meets and saves man through confronting him with the biblical message of salvation. (b) The unity and purpose of the biblical message come to focus in Jesus Christ; he is the perspective by which the Bible may be interpreted. (c) There is in the Bible an authority for Christian education which prevents the "use" of the Bible for objectives arrived at independently of the nature of the biblical witness; the Bible points to and mediates the authority of God through and within the Christian community. (d) Similarly, the Bible is more than a resource among other resources; it may become a channel for encounter with God. (e) Results of biblical scholarship are, and must be, recognized and taken into account in preparation of subject matter and in curriculum planning.

Although certain contemporary writers still view the Bible in terms of its evolutionary unity, and see it as a resource, many other current writings dealing with philosophy of Christian education are in basic agreement with the points just listed. Howard Grimes probably reflects most clearly the consensus existing among Christian educators, and in his drawing upon the results of ecumenical studies for principles of biblical interpretation he directly relates Christian education to current biblical scholarship.[96] Another writer, a theologian making a contribution to Christian education, reflects and unifies in a rather remarkable way what theologians and educators are saying today about revelation and the biblical witness. Allen Miller's book, *Invitation to Theology*,[97] presents a covenant theology built around the concept of the divine-human covenant drama.

Moving back from the area of agreement to variations in views, it should be stated that differences seem to be primarily in terms of emphasis and terminology. Smart speaks in even firmer tones of the determinative role of the Bible for Christian education than do Miller and Sherrill, both of whom recognize its key importance. Miller moves more to the Bible from experience in defining the Bible's place in Christian education, seeing it as resource and yet more than resource. Perhaps this is because of his understanding of revelation as being more determinative of how content is used than of what content is chosen, of the process through which change occurs than of the necessity of teaching a particular theological system. The role Sherrill assigns to the Bible seems to emerge from a dialogue between theology and the social sciences, between the nature of the Bible and the life of the Christian community, and to be subject to change depending on changes in the situation.

Smart's concept of the Bible as the Word of God points to a unity of the biblical message, whereas Miller's and Sherrill's views allow more room for diversity within a basic unity. Moreover, it ascribes to the Bible a *sole* authority which is more a *supreme* authority for other thinkers in the field, although there is agreement that ultimately all authority is of God. All three men recognize the necessity for biblical scholarship; Sherrill recognizes more clearly than the other two the dangers inherent in an uncritical use of the "results" of biblical criticism. Differences in formulation of the biblical message are reflected in the terms "Word of God," "themes," and "drama." Other minor differences need not be noted here.

Whatever differences in approach may exist, the important fact is that Christian educators seem to be cognizant of the crucial significance of the Bible for Christian education, and to be seeking to formulate their philosophy in terms that take into account that significance.

V The Relevance of the Bible

Biblical scholars who have been concerned lest outmoded thought forms and obscure language of the Bible might make it seem irrelevant to life today have proposed various solutions for the problem, ranging all the way from Bultmann's demythologizing to Anderson's admonition to "sit where these ancient people sat and learn to look at the human scene from their unique point of view."[1] Christian educators, too, have tried many approaches to making the Bible relevant. Sometimes teachers have been instructed to "teach as Jesus taught" or children to "be friendly like David," and the Bible has seemed relevant by virtue of the examples it offered both for moral living and for all manner of activities.

Another approach has been to study man and his needs and find help for him in biblical answers. In curriculum construction this has frequently meant the use of "pupil-centered" units of study, beginning with life situations which have led back to the Bible; or sometimes, in "content" units, there has been a conscious effort to have a time of "application" for every Bible lesson studied. Often this has resulted in more attention to ethical instruction than to consideration of the heart of the gospel message, and the question of the essential relevance of the Bible has increasingly been raised in recent years. Is relevance primarily at the point where the gospel touches man at the deepest level of his existence? Or is it at the level of conduct? If it is at a deeper level than conduct, then where and how is man to find guidance for concrete decisions day by day? And what is the educator to suggest to teachers for study Sunday by Sunday?

Not all these questions have been answered, and even in the answers currently being offered by the same three writers previously considered there is considerable divergence of opinion.

God Speaks

Because it is God who speaks through the Bible, and because his word is always a word of salvation, the Bible is revelant, according to James Smart. Without this word, man would be alone, "that is, cut off from God and from his fellow man," and so "deprived of his existence."[2] A moralistic education is always inadequate; one must go beyond to the message of the gospel and to a Christian understanding of man before the Bible can be used in a context where it achieves its true relevance.

The Veil of Moralism

Smart's *bête noire* is the moralistic approach to the Bible "which turns every passage merely into an occasion for moralizing," and puts "a veil over it that conceals its true meaning and makes it essentially uninteresting." This makes the Bible into a "gallery of saints, good people whom we are to admire and imitate," and necessitates "a little whitewashing."[3] According to Smart, of all the failures of religious education in the past—and most of the past may be characterized as failure—nothing has been more devastating than concentration on good conduct. The pathetic, hilarious, and shameless distortion of the Bible brought about by casting over it "the suffocating fog of moralism" is to be found in both conservative and liberal church schools.[4]

But the time has come to change all this, according to Smart. The goal of character development is a legalistic repudiation of the doctrine of justification by faith, and must be radically redefined to direct attention to God's action in a way that calls people to yield themselves wholly to his sovereignty.

Kerygma and Didache

A contributing factor to the development of moralism in teaching, as Smart sees it, has been C. H. Dodd's distinction between *kerygma* and *didache*. "Much harm" has been done by a wide acceptance of views which lend themselves easily to a detachment of teaching "from all essential relation to the *kerygma*."[5] Actually the entire biblical tradition, although recognizing a difference in teaching and preaching, assumes that both "endeavor at every point . . . to gain a hearing for the good news that in Jesus Christ the time is fulfilled, the Kingdom is at hand, so that every man may repent and believe."[6] Dodd has performed a service in reminding the pulpit that the *kerygma* "was the indispensable essence of the Church's original preaching."[7] On the other hand, teaching, as *didache*, has often floundered in isolation from the *kerygma*. Upon Dodd's interpretation, "they cease to have a single content and to be parallel services which the Church renders to one and the same word of God." What he has done is to say that Acts 5:42 means that "the apostles 'preached Jesus Christ and taught Christian ethics,' instead of what is written: 'They ceased not to teach and preach Jesus Christ.' "[8]

What Smart seems to be suggesting is that the essential relevance of the Bible lies in the *kerygma*, whereas religious educators have been seeking to find the relevance in ethical instruction, in *didache*. Yet relevance is actually accomplished only when the two are seen together. Preaching needs the "more open and vulnerable situation" of teaching.[9] Isolated proclamation, a declaration of the Word of God in sermons, suffers from a lack of intimate knowledge of what is happening in people's lives. From the point of view of Christian education, however, a recognition that the basic content of the *kerygma* and *didache* is the same, though expressed differently, is one of the first steps toward greater effectiveness in teaching.

The Christian Doctrine of Man

If the Bible has significance for man, then it must be related to his needs, and this necessitates an understanding of who man is and what he is like. It is therefore essential that a program of Christian education operate on the basis of "a Christian doctrine of man."[10]

The key word in what Smart says is "Christian." It points to the inadequacy of discovery from the secular field of the needs of various age groups. A curriculum built upon needs "is in danger of becoming a very thin and watery curriculum, particularly if much weight is allowed to what the child himself conceives to be his needs."[11] Indeed, the Christian understanding of what it means to be a person is based on revelation, and therefore on the Bible. "The starting point for a Christian in his definition of true humanity is Jesus Christ. He is, for us, not only the revelation of the nature of God but also the revelation of the nature of man."[12] But what is seen in Jesus Christ is not what is seen in oneself or in one's fellow man. What happened, according to the Scriptures, is that man sinned against God, and "in isolation from God he quickly loses his humanity."[13] Looking at himself in the light of Jesus Christ, man sees his own propensity toward self-centeredness and his involvement in the sinfulness of humanity. The knowledge of God in Jesus Christ reveals man's greatest need—a way to become what God intended him to be. It is only through the Christian revelation that this knowledge of need comes, and if the Christian faith is to be relevant, it must speak to this need.

The revelation which brings knowledge of sin at the same time brings knowledge of grace. Through Jesus Christ, judgment and mercy come together. Man's lost humanity is restored, and he receives as God's gift the power of being transformed into the likeness of Jesus Christ. In him, man is brought back into relationship with God and with neighbor, and becomes a new being, living with "God as the sovereign center of his being."[14]

This is not to say that Smart disregards scientific research in psychology. It is to say that such findings are not the basis for Christian education, and that what counts is "what God thinks" of men, not what they "think of themselves."[15] The Bible bears witness to "God's mind" concerning men and their actions, and to God's work in the lives of men to achieve his purpose for them. If man is to fulfill his destiny, then he must look to the Bible for his understanding of a life lived each moment "out of the infinite resources of God," as was the life of Jesus Christ.[16]

The Nature of True Relevance

If the Bible shows man what he is, and what he may become, holding out to him hope and power for that becoming, it is relevant. "The ultimate question is not, Can this individual find a solution to his immediate problem? but rather, Can this individual find the destiny God has for him in Jesus Christ, and can he find his place in the Church of God?"[17] Men are not to imitate Moses, but to see how in all the events of his life "the hand of God was directing him toward his true destiny."[18] The responsibility of the educator is not discharged by having a unit of study on the Bible, and then one on "life problems." Somehow a way must be found to bring the two together, focusing the Bible upon the "actualities of the modern world" so that it becomes "a revelation for now."[19]

Yet the Bible does not offer easy answers to specific questions, making it possible to view the Christian life as a succession of moral acts, each an entity within itself. Instead, the Christian life is a response of obedience to the Word of God in the entirety of life, including the concrete situations of daily living. This is the totalitarian claim the Bible makes upon human life, and it is at the same time the offer of the gift of fullness of life and perfect freedom to be found only in subjection to God.

The Relationship Between God and Man

The Bible is relevant both at the ultimate level of man's existence and throughout all the stages of development of his growth toward mature Christian faith. Whereas James Smart's emphasis is on the former, Randolph Crump Miller brings the two together in a sacramental view of life which emphasizes the meaning of redemption *now*. It is because man's great need for redemption and God's purpose of redemption coalesce in the biblical account of the "relationships between a divine personal being and human persons"[20] that the Bible is relevant for today's world. It "tells a story that reveals to man both the meaning of his condition and the possibility of being healed."[21]

Man does not see this automatically. He does not perceive the meaning in God's action, nor realize that the drama of redemption continues, calling for his participation. Thus *the major task of Christian education today is to discover and impart the relevance of Christian truth.*"[22] This involves at least three things: theology formulated as "the truth-about-God-in-relation-to-man" as the basis for Christian education; the drama of redemption interpreted in terms of the God-man relationships for every age; and an indication of how the Bible, coming into form through the life of the church, actually becomes relevant for persons who participate in that life.

Theology and Relevance

Theology suggests relationships. Miller hopes to "keep the problem of relevance in mind by defining theology as 'the truth-about-God-in-relation-to-man,' which means that we discover God at work in history and in our own generation, and especially in our own daily relationships."[23] This is why theology affects Christian education. Education takes formulations of truths from the past and makes them the basis of experiences by which truth in the present may be known; "these truths *are* theology, but theology becomes relevant only as the learner recognizes his basic needs in the perspective of God's activity in his experience."[24]

In *The Clue to Christian Education* it was Miller's purpose to show how Christian education could take place as theology was placed in the background and then interpreted in terms of relationships experienced by the various ages. Concerned "that the Bible itself illuminate the relationships of daily living in terms of the resources of the Gospel," Miller wrote *Biblical Theology and Christian Education.*[25] "From the standpoint of Biblical theology," he says, "we need to examine the acts of God in the processes of history and then to see how these events can be made relevant to boys and girls, men and women, of the twentieth century."[26] This means going beyond a facing of "problems of meaning and relevance . . . in terms of selecting the most appropriate Bible passages for the age of the child." What is involved is having a *"basis in theology* for a perspective from which to teach." This makes it possible to ask and seek an answer for the basic question in regard to the relevance of the Bible: *"What is the meaning and relevance of the Gospel in its wholeness to the situation in which the particular learner now exists?"*[27]

The Drama of Redemption

What Miller was doing in analyzing biblical events in terms of drama was not solely a study of the structure of the Bible. He was seeking to make the Bible relevant, to recast biblical theology so as to demonstrate the correlation between biblical and contemporary "relationships." As he sees it, the result of the formulation of biblical theology in terms of drama, proceeding from the assumption that even "the newborn babe is within the drama of redemption from the moment of his conception,"[28] is an elimination of many of the educational difficulties attendant upon teaching the Bible, particularly to young children. "The drama tells the story of everyman. The basic relationships it describes are as true for a child as for an adult. The great events are those of our common experience."[29] A rather extensive passage is quoted here to point up the parallels between this "common experience" of mankind and the five acts of the biblical drama.

> Every child is created, and in the experience of birth and early experiences as an infant he is faced with his creaturehood and his need for autonomy in the midst of dependence and security. He is faced by the rigidity of the adult world, the rule of law, and the dependability of discipline. He needs redemption, for he cannot save himself; and in his helplessness and reliance on his parents in whom he lives and moves and has his being, he must be saved from death if he is to live. Except he live in community, he cannot become a person; for community, communion, and communi-

cation go together. Through the community of home, school, and church channels are opened for the Holy Spirit. And from the time he is weaned, he faces judgment, even though it be only his mother's disapproval as he fails to perform according to her expectations.[30]

This summary can only be suggestive of Miller's full treatment, for he shows how "the Biblical drama applies at every age, according to the capacities and experiences of that age."[31] Whereas Anderson enjoins people to re-enter the biblical world, identifying with the characters so as to experience the drama from their perspective, Miller's approach seems to be more a bringing of the biblical drama to the modern world, focusing on using biblical insights to interpret present experience and thus to find direction for living.

To relate the Bible to life today is the educational task, as Miller sees it. And the important thing to note is that because the biblical drama is "a true revelation of God at work in history, it is dynamic and relevant as God is at work in us."[32] Thus this statement might be made: "The whole Bible is always relevant, even when particular parts of the Bible are not."[33]

The Bible and the Church

The biblical drama cannot become relevant except through the life of the church. This statement rests basically on the assumption that there is a "theology of the Bible" which becomes relevant through the "language of relationships" within the church. This "language of relationships" becomes most meaningful when it is placed within the framework of the unfolding drama of the Bible, worked out in detail by Miller in his book of sermons, *The Symphony of the Christian Year,* as well as in *Biblical Theology and Christian Education.* Thus indirectly he shows the possibility of relating teaching, preaching, and the drama of the church year with the drama of the Bible.

Another reason the Bible and the church must be seen together insofar as relevance is concerned is that a person living today *enters* Act IV (Church) of the drama. Every person may experience one or all of the acts simultaneously. He may be existing primarily in one act rather than in another. This must be kept in mind always. But regardless of where he is in his personal development, the *perspective* must always be that of Act IV.

The life of the Christian man lived in Act IV is a life of response to the totality of God's action. Christian education therefore cannot be only moral or character education. Smart speaks of moralism as resulting in use of the Bible in "snippets." Miller speaks of "tidbits of theology," and *"hors d'oeuvres* of Biblical verses,"[34] and says that the "admonition to 'be like Jesus' is silly."[35] Instead, the ethical life is "a man's total response to God in the situation in which he finds himself."[36] The whole of life is one's vocation, and all behavior has a religious dimension. Specific decisions come from within a relationship to Jesus Christ within the "community of the Holy Spirit."[37]

Practically, from the point of view of curriculum construction, this means that curriculum centers around *"a twofold relationship between God and the learner,"* and is *"both God-centered and experience-centered."*[38] Experiences are brought into the light of the gospel. "The Church is always on the sidelines, making use of whatever experiences the home and school and community provide for a Christian interpretation of life."[39]

Upon no point is Miller more positive than that of the relevance of the Bible and theology to life. What may be said, in summary, is that the Bible, in the very nature of its witness, *is* relevant; it *becomes* relevant as persons move into the drama of redemption and are enabled to see the meaning of what is going on. And here again event and interpretation constitute revelation.

Predicament and Theme

The gospel of the Kingdom of God in its wholeness speaks to every aspect of man's predicament of being lost, of needing salvation. The method by which Lewis Sherrill seeks to expound this general relevance of the Bible in more specific terms stems from his principle of correspondence, which eventuates in an analysis of the human situation and of the biblical message in terms of predicament and theme, which are in correlation. The relevance thus demonstrated is by nature internal rather than external, and points to an ethical life that is truly Christian as resulting from a relationship with God.

The Principle of Correspondence

"When we ask what the relevance of the Bible is," Sherrill says, "we are really asking what the relevance of revelation is." And the answer is that relevance *"lies in the fact that the disclosure fits the need."*[40]

Such a statement leads to the establishment of what may be called "the principle of correspondence between divine revelation and human need."[41] This principle is close to Tillich's "method of correlation." Sherrill says that the methods are similar but not identical. They are agreed in the recognition of the mutuality between revelation and human need, but different in that Sherrill makes "the mutuality *personal* to a degree which Professor Tillich does not seem prepared to affirm."[42] On this point Sherrill says he is closer to Farmer and to Howe than to Tillich. The Bible witnesses both to the personal nature of the relationship between God and man, and to "the correspondence between man's persisting need and God's revelation of himself."[43]

The Bible is relevant at every level in the religious development of the person, confronting him with questions which must be answered in his maturing selfhood if he is to move to the next higher level. Along with relevant answers, it also provides the power of God's Spirit to appropriate these answers. The whole book, *The Struggle of the Soul,* illustrates this correspondence between man's developmental needs and God's revelation. Even the structure of the Bible shows the parallel between the history of Israel and of the church, and God's action. From whatever angle the matter is approached, therefore, it may be said that "the basic principle of correspondence means that whatever the particular shape of the circumstances that threaten him, man is not forsaken in the dangers that surround him."[44]

Three questions may be asked to help clarify the way in which Sherrill works out details of the church's use of the Bible in the light of the "principle of correspondence." Since the Bible offers both questions and answers, does one confine study in the church to Bible materials? Does one begin with the themes of the Bible or with man's predicament? What does this have to suggest as to problem-centered versus Bible-centered teaching?

With reference to the first question, Sherrill holds that "the Bible is the principal source from which the church's teaching is drawn."[45] It is not the only source, however. There is a legitimate place for "an immense range of materials"—biography, history, drama, a very "embarrassment of riches."[46] Exactly what this place is, and by what standard other materials are to be selected, are subjects not covered by Sherrill.

As to the second question, it may be said that it is possible to begin with either revelational themes or human need, and there are values in each approach. But the emphasis on confrontation means that "we do not understand learning to be merely or even chiefly a matter of searching for truth. For there is a sense in which truth faces us, presents itself to us, and does so whether we ask for it or not, whether we feel the need for it or not."[47] Perhaps this is the reason he sees the use of themes as "especially promising" as a beginning.[48] And seeing the interrelationship of themes moving toward unity and climax in the incarnation and passion of Jesus Christ overcomes fragmentation and prepares the way for the appropriation of revelation.

What has just been said is indicative of Sherrill's attitude toward the third question concerning "problem-centered" teaching, which he sees as a "nightmare of trying to permit a curriculum to grow up entirely out of the questions which children are now asking and the needs they now feel."[49] This is rather strong language for Sherrill; it is critically directed toward efforts to "make" the Bible relevant whether it is or not, to force it to become "a handbook" or "a sourcebook," and thus to miss the element of depth in human need.[50] To balance his statement, it is essential to understand that "the materials drawn from the Bible to be used in the Christian community should be chosen with the anxiety and the predicaments of the people of our own time in view," and that the "hunger at this point" must lead educators always to keep in mind men's deep question of "whether the Bible has any word to speak to their condition."[51]

Man's Predicament

Sherrill's use of the term "predicament" is intended to designate a depth that goes beyond what the terms "need" and "problem" ordinarily connote. The sense of predicament may be observable as specific needs or problems which "take their particular shape for individual selves because the deep underlying anxiety has been stirred up by threats to the existing self." One cannot deal with these needs as specifics without running the risk of ignoring their rootage in a more profound anxiety.[52]

How does one arrive at an understanding of this deep-seated predicament of man? There are at least two ways which are to be employed in conjunction with each other. One is the analysis of human need by the use of "such techniques as are familiar in sociological and psychological studies."[53] When Sherrill employs these techniques, as he does in the first part of *The Gift of Power,* he concludes that man has the capacity "for closeness, for liberation, for community, for individuality, for wholeness, for creativity, and for growth," but that *"every point in the foundations of selfhood is under threat."*[54] The other way of understanding predicament is to study the biblical account, which points to *both* need and its healing. The Christian religion, which recognizes the tragedy of man's predicament, also "understands how tragedy can be transcended."[55]

Whichever way the analysis is made, it will eventuate in the setting forth of those aspects of man's predicament which, in accordance with the principle of correspondence, will correlate with the great themes of revelation. This is the essence of Sherrill's understanding of the relevance of the Bible. It is, perhaps, a way of overcoming the dichotomy between "problem-centered" and "Bible-centered" teaching, precisely because predicament and theme *belong* together.

Internal Relevance

A basic assumption for all that has been said is that Sherrill understands relevance of the Bible to be internal rather than external in nature. That is to say, the relevance of the Bible is not to be found in terms of legalism, "trying to settle intricate ethical problems by appealing to particular Biblical passages, much as one would cite a statute in a code of law." Here the Bible is "the master of men."[56] Nor is it to be found in terms of mere practicalism, calling upon the Bible as an oracle for answers to specific questions which men formulate from their "felt need." Here man is "the master of the Bible."[57] Both these approaches tend in the direction of seeing an "external" relevance in the Bible. They are a part of man's age-long search for relevance, a search which has led to many "distorted forms," but which "must go on in each generation."[58]

Even the fragmenting of the church's work in recent years, Sherrill says, was "a groping for a sense of relevance and practicality, especially in the American churches." Europeans thought it was "mere activism," whereas "it was a characteristically American way of trying to regain contact between the church and the people."[59] The effort of Sunday school teachers to give guidance in matters of conduct was and often is a search for relevance. But all of this is in terms of external relevance, whereas actually it is not necessary "that every portion of Biblical material used should be turned in the direction of a 'conduct outcome.' "[60]

Although it is not possible entirely to separate external from internal relevance, and although both forms can be found in the Bible, Sherrill considers that it is of basic importance to "seek the principle of relevance primarily in terms of internal relevance," which means a focusing of attention on the "points at which revelation bears directly upon the situation of the existing human self."[61] This in turn leads back to the thought of relevance in terms of the "principle of correspondence," of predicament and theme, of call and answer. In every case, relevance touches the self at the deepest level of existence. The question thus arises concerning the nature of the ethical life of the Christian. Perhaps in simplest terms it might be said that "a man in fellowship with God has the responsibility of determining his own conduct in the light of that fellowship."[62] This fellowship, which makes possible the life of faith, designated either as "life in Christ" or "life in the Spirit," results in an ever-deepening "interpenetration" between "the divine Self and the human self."[63]

Ethical teaching and proclamation cannot be separated. Sherrill sees the distinction between *kerygma* and *didache* not so much in terms of differences in content as of differences in emphasis in the historical development of Jesus' ministry. The earlier part, according to Sherrill's analysis of the Gospels, was characterized by preaching and evangelizing, by a call to repentance and a proclamation of glad tidings directed toward developing faith in "the deep places of the soul."[64] Even there, however, teaching was to be found; evidently Jesus "felt impelled to follow the preaching and the evangelizing immediately with teaching." Otherwise, distorted ideas of the Kingdom would have developed.[65] But after Peter's confession, Jesus "is not again spoken of in the Gospels as preaching . . . for the perfectly natural reason that what he had been proclaiming had now come to pass and was beginning to be acknowledged."[66] The disciples assumed the work of preaching and evangelizing. Jesus' own ministry passed into another phase, the teaching ministry, which extended almost to the very end. The teaching moved "into new depths" as Jesus opened "more fully the meaning and cost of discipleship."[67] Then both preaching and teaching were absorbed and climaxed in the events of the Passion and Resurrection.

What Sherrill seems to be saying, then, is that ethical teaching and gospel proclamation are both essential and are interdependent, but that the emphasis comes at the point of where a person is in his religious development. There is to be no arbitrary division of the two, and no establishing of superior or inferior values.

Moreover, while the *basis* of the ethical life is the relationship with God through faith, it does not follow that the church has no concern with the specifics of conduct, or that it does not deal directly with such specifics. Although he does not develop the statement, Sherrill says that it is "always immediately clear that the right of the 'spiritual community' to set up limitations and controls is not only recognized but urged; and broad suggestions as to 'spiritual' and 'fleshly' types of conduct are freely made" in the Bible.[68] At the same time he recognizes the need for "controls," Sherrill calls upon the church to "press the responsibility for decisions in matters of ethical conduct back upon the individual."[69] As the individual seeks to settle issues as they arise (and they cannot be settled before),[70] and does so from the perspective of his "life in Christ," he finds that the life of fellowship with God is also the life of freedom under God.[71] He has been given no blueprint of the will of God, but he is given "the life-long task of discovering how love may best govern him in his own living."[72]

Summary

On the basic issue of relevance there is no hint of disagreement among the three writers considered. Relevance is not external. It is not to be understood in terms of specifics, of analogous situations, of easy application of principles to conduct. When this is realized, educators are released from what Paul H. Vieth says has often been "an uneasy feeling that any venture into Christian ethical life had to be sanctioned and hallowed by some tie-up to a Bible story or Bible passage." It has made unnecessary the "fantastic applications of Scripture to fit cases for which there could be no Scripture parallel," and it has made possible the "free exploration" of the relation of Christian convictions to "the problems of living."[73]

On the other hand, relevance *is* internal. It lies in the gospel, at the deepest level of existence—what a man is and may become as God's redemptive purpose for him is realized. Again referring to Vieth for a concise summary, it may be said that "man's experience of salvation through God's love should lead naturally to thankful response in life which is pleasing to God." Ethical emphasis must never be separated from "the prior consideration of man's responsibility to God which gives it meaning."[74] The Christian life, viewed as response to God, as a life transformed from within and empowered by the grace of God through his indwelling Spirit, means that man has heard and responded to the Word of God, that he has entered into the drama of redemption within which decisions are made and salvation appropriated day by day, that he has found in God the answer to his predicament of being lost. Because the Bible confronts man with the Word of God, because it calls him to participate in the drama it records, because through its gospel message it prepares the way for encounter with God, it is relevant.

Other writers who have dealt directly with the problem of relevance would be in basic agreement with this summary. Reuel Howe has made a significant contribution to the understanding of relevance. His method, which sees the correlation between man's need and God's action, places him alongside Sherrill in his approach.[75] Clarence Tucker Craig makes a special contribution in his view that there are two definable uses of the Bible. These two uses become clear only after it is recognized that Christianity is "gospel" rather than "quest." The first use is *the presentation of the gospel faith.*[76] The second use is concerned with *"the ethical response to the gospel."*[77] Having begun with the "given," the *gospel,* one would move to the second use of the Bible in the *quest* for the meaning of that gospel in life. Reason, one's own past experience and that of other persons, various methods of communicating with one another, all may play a role in the "quest."

In spite of the basic agreement on the nature of relevance, there are differences in terminology and in biblical analysis as a means of putting relevance in manageable terms. The more important differences are in the area of the beginning point for Christian teaching. For Smart, the beginning point is primarily the Bible. For Miller, it is experience. For Sherrill, there is a tendency toward beginning with the gospel or the themes of the Bible, but his method of correlation suggests the possibility of beginning at either point.

Smart's approach to *kerygma* and *didache,* in relation to Christian teaching, is more in terms of content analysis, while Sherrill's is more in terms of their historical function in the ministry of Jesus. In view of the fact that the search for relevance has often resulted in a fragmenting of the Bible, the question might be raised whether such would be the case in any of the three positions considered here. An answer is difficult, because fragmentation occurs at the level of curriculum construction, which is a step beyond the writings of the three men. Smart's concept of the "Word of God" and his emphasis on the unity of revelation in the Bible make it hard to suppose that he would permit the use of the Bible in "snippets," although he gives fewer particulars of biblical analysis or implications of relevance than either Miller or Sherrill. Miller's "drama" approach has the value of giving historical continuity to the Bible story, and of giving an individual a chronological rootedness in Act IV as a perspective within which the relevance could be worked out in whatever stage of individual development he might be. Whether Sherrill's use of "themes" would result in fragmentation is difficult to say. That seems possible, though such is certainly not his intention. And the approach emphasizes the relevance of the gospel to each individual, regardless of where he is in his spiritual development.

More work needs to be done, therefore, on the practical level of helping persons know how to teach session by session, but profound contributions have been made by these writers whose different approaches enrich the whole field of thought regarding the relevance of the Bible.

VI | The Appropriation of the Biblical Message

The current emphasis on the sovereignty of God, with the accompanying lessened confidence in man and his ability, might seem to suggest that there is nothing man can do to bring about his own or another's entry into and growth in the Christian life. Appropriation of the biblical message would seem to lie beyond his powers. Indeed, since revelation is the self-communication of God, and as such is the living dynamic constituting the biblical message, it would appear axiomatic that communication rests entirely in the hands of God. At the same time, educators are criticized for their failures to "produce" genuine Christians and for their ineffectual methodology accompanied by incorrect theology, resulting in illiteracy so far as the Bible is concerned.

The assumption seems to be that man's activity makes at least some difference. Thus, while it is agreed that man cannot control, manipulate, or assuredly effect reception of that message, some participation in God's plan is possible, and is even required. God's willingness and intention to use human channels of communication lays upon man a responsibility for finding his role.

What are the various approaches among Christian educators to understanding both God's role and man's? How does appropriation of the biblical message take place? Three key words, confrontation, participation, and encounter, suggest the distinctive perspectives of Smart, Miller, and Sherrill.

Appropriation and Confrontation

What God's role is stands out clearly so far as James Smart is concerned, and is quite consistent with the whole of his theological or philosophical position. God is God, and sets a question mark against the whole of man's existence. That question mark, that confrontation of man by God, necessitates decision; repentance holds the possibility of change. Were it not for God's initiative in confronting man through his self-revelation, bringing a new knowledge offering only the alternatives of acceptance or rejection, there would be no possibility of appropriation of the biblical message. Yet when the response is acceptance, the power inherent in the message gives birth to a new life within the person thus confronted. In a sense, then, confrontation cannot be separated from appropriation, and all is of God.

Man's role as educator is less clear-cut. Smart specifically states, however, that "revelation itself demands a human channel of communication."[1] That human channel is designated as the church, and an imperative is laid upon the educator to bestir himself, even though the forms of his activities are not specified in detail, for "teaching belongs to the essence of the Church."[2] By inference from Smart's position in general, perhaps it might be said that here, too, the form of the activity is a response that depends upon the nature of the message. At any rate, the educator is to work through the church, teaching in a way that anticipates conversion, and that recognizes human limitations while trusting in God.

Appropriation as Response

When man is confronted by God, his response of commitment is itself the appropriation of the biblical message. Response, decision, faithfulness—these are terms which characterize appropriation for Smart. A classic example both of appropriation and of its fruits may be observed in the Reformation, where in the beginning a few men, "quietly reading the Scriptures and delving into them in earnest," were captivated by the truth they found there. This truth "transformed their personal lives and remolded their entire spiritual outlook."[3] The firm convictions these men developed about the true nature of Christianity led them to raise a protest *for* the truth. The transformation that took place, both in individual lives and in the church, was response. There are at least four important implications arising from such an under-standing.

The most obvious point has been made repeatedly, because whatever Smart is discussing he never fails to see the importance of the Bible. He follows the Reformation tradition in assigning the Bible a pre-eminent place, convinced, as were the Reformers, that an understanding of the biblical message is the first essential for preservation and growth of the church. Something happens today, as then, through the instrumentality of the Bible which happens through no other book. "Its unique claim is that in it God speaks to man and God comes to man."[4] Whether ordinary men need more help in understanding what is meant by "God speaks," or whether false expectations are aroused in young people who are assured that in the Bible "God speaks as person to person,"[5] or whether even Christians may conceivably need some way of arriving at concrete decisions and some description of the form of the ethical life demanded as response to God's speaking—these are not the issues, for Smart. Nothing more basic can be said about the Christian life than the fact that the Bible is the Word of God.

This points to the importance of belief in shaping conduct. "Our thoughts and ideas and beliefs determine the nature of our characters and give the pattern to our conduct."[6] That is why the neglect of the "knowledge" side of religion in recent years is so serious. It has led to a dependence upon conscience as "a sufficient source for knowing the will of God," when the actual fact is that "it is in the nature of conscience that uninstructed it cannot speak."[7] Moreover, it has led to an incoherence among Christian people today which is deplorable. Even virtue without knowledge which can be formulated into communicable words is inadequate, because the "utterance" of faith is the means of witnessing. Articulation of one's faith seems necessary for its appropriation for oneself, and for one's fulfillment of his responsibility to witness to others.

However, the emphasis on belief does not preclude the right and the need to doubt. Man cannot in this life escape wholly from unbelief, any more than he can escape wholly from sin. He is saved by the grace of God, not by adherence to right doctrine. Neither man nor church is wholly redeemed. Both are being redeemed.

A recognition of the right to honest doubt is related to the overwhelming conclusion that the role of the educator is to grant freedom to the biblical message. That is to say, where response is appropriation, the need is to point to the message and to get rid of all impediments that may prevent its standing forth in clarity and confrontation. Educators do not determine response in advance, nor manipulate people. The assumption that one can develop "a technique for producing Christians" is "blasphemous."[8]

Moreover, any rigid predetermined objective or picture of "a certain type" of Christian is as debilitating as is a civilization's education of persons "who can be depended upon to think the right things, say the right things, and fight for the right things."[9] What is sought is not conformity, but aliveness to the truth. "The fact that God chose to come to man in a word has in it an infinite respect for the freedom and integrity of the human person. God is not willing to compel faith or obedience in any man."[10] The same must be true for the educator.

The Church as Human Channel of Communication

Whatever happens through confrontation or by way of Christian education happens through the witness of the church which proclaims and teaches the Word of God, according to Smart. The church is both divine and human. Although the human elements can never be ultimately determinative of communication (which implies reception and response), they do somehow make a difference. *Just* how is not delineated by Smart, but it is assumed. Negatively speaking, for example, the current disinclination of religious educators "to set their collective house in order theologically"[11] and to rethink "every aspect of the work of Christian education" creates a "dangerously false situation" and "bodes ill for the future."[12] Or again approaching the matter negatively, on a more practical level, the failure of religious education to deal adequately with problems attendant upon the use of the Bible in the church school accounts at least in part for the fact that it has not been more effective in the lives of people. Men have often muffled God's speaking instead of helping it come through clearly.

What are some of these failures of the past? Smart points to several.[13] The presentation to the pupil of the Bible "arranged under subjects" has resulted in a fragmentation which gives no grasp of the Bible as a whole. There has been a failure to give a solid historical framework and background, or to use vivid historical imagination in dissolving "the atmosphere of unreality that clings about the Bible." The dangers in the moralistic approach have already been indicated. Many children have been exposed to too much Bible too young, and others have been victims of the assumption that only certain portions were suitable for each age group; both extremes point to the need for proper grading. Not enough understanding has been given of the variety of literary forms in the Bible. The failure to study "the peculiar language of the Bible," its strange thought forms, has made men lose contact with the reality implied in words like judgment and salvation. Finally, lack of a real purpose in teaching the Bible has often resulted in merely giving information about it.

Human failures in all these areas have had detrimental influences. Much of what Smart says critically is generalization, and some of his positive suggestions thrown in here and there have actually been used repeatedly in the past. Perhaps, however, these past efforts have themselves been too fragmentary to be of much significance.

Failures point to still unsolved problems about the use of the Bible in the church school, and hint at the possibility that man may be an aid instead of a hindrance in the process of communication. Smart makes a positive suggestion about grading as indeed making a difference, especially when one considers how small children have been frightened by Abraham's having to leave home or how Noah has been relegated to the kindergarten when adults in an Atomic Age teetering "on the brink of self-destruction" need desperately the significance in his story.[14] All of this means that there must be "constant experiment to find what parts of Scripture can be taught most effectively to each age group" and that the church "can learn much from secular education in this matter of grading and should be alert to keep pace in religious training with the mental development of the child in public school."[15]

There are other questions which educators frequently ask one another about communicating the gospel. What about appropriate methods? Smart hardly mentions this. One would assume that he would lean strongly toward instruction or indoctrination, though in such a way as to respect the person being instructed. He points out that although giving information is not enough, the teaching of facts is essential.[16] Facts in their setting must be known before they can be interpreted for the modern situation. Instruction does not necessarily mean *telling* people, however. Smart sees the need for a "wide variety of approaches" on the adult level, and recognizes the potentialities in small study groups or certain types of ministerial sermon-lectures.[17]

What about the role of reason and the relation of experience to learning? Little is said directly about either. Certainly reason can never discover God, but it has a place in responding to him.

> There has been far too much pious sentimentalism and what is called the devotional approach to the study of the Bible, and not enough hardheaded, thorough delving into it, to get at the truth which it contains, in which alone our generation, or any other generation, can find the clue to the solution of the dilemmas of its existence.[18]

If "delving" into the contents of the Bible is the use of reason, Smart seems to be suggesting the possibility that reason has a role in appropriation and in reaching ethical decisions about particular problems in today's world, although the position is not developed.

Insofar as the relation of experience to learning is concerned, experience does not lead to God and it is not the beginning point for curriculum construction, but it is the place where education becomes meaningful, for "education begins with the child's first experience of the meaning of life."[19] This indicates the importance of "a close co-ordination between the courses studied in the church school and the present life experience of the pupil."[20] In relation to experience, Christian education can "provide the light in which the situations of life take on their true Christian meaning and the pupil finds, in the Christian faith, the key to the mystery of life."[21] That key is to be found in the Bible, with the aid of competent teachers.

These matters relate primarily to the church school, one of the three major agencies of Christian education. The other two are the church as a whole and the home. In the Christian home, founded by God in the divine order of his creation as the basic unit of all human society, it is possible for the child to be led "to look beyond the parent to the God whom the parent unashamedly serves."[22]

In the church as a whole the Bible comes alive and its message lives. Indeed, in his belief that the whole church educates, Smart is most positive about human participation in communication. "The primary educational force, which forms the background for all else that is said and done, is the impact of the total Church upon the lives of children and youth."[23]

The structure of a church's program includes five elements, as Smart sees it: education in the Scriptures, worship, fellowship, growth into the "Church of the ages" (involving study of church history), and training to be the church "in the world of today" (involving exercise of discipleship now).[24] In a church where all these elements are found, one can "escape from abstractions" and find a "concreteness" in the whole process of Christian education.[25] Perhaps it might be inferred also that in a community like this the Christian gospel could more readily be communicated.

Conversion

When one starts from the premise that God's revelation of himself is confrontation of man, as Smart does, and when this is coupled with the biblical understanding of man as sinner, the conclusion is that conversion is essential. This does not mean that one is first a child of sin and then, by a sudden conversion, becomes a child of God. No matter how deeply a man has fallen into sin, "beneath it all he is a child of God."[26] Even the child born into a Christian home cannot simply "grow" into the Kingdom. He and his "good" Christian family may find it hard to understand sin and the need for repentance, having "actually substituted a very smug middle-class form of religion and morality for New Testament Christianity."[27] Conversion, then, always has a place in Christian education, but the term is not to be interpreted narrowly. Rather, it describes "the transformation which takes place in our human life with each fresh inbreaking of God upon us."[28]

This view does not see conversion as antithetical to moral and spiritual growth. Transformation of life is always the expectation of the teacher of the gospel, although that transformation is not under his control. His role is that of giving the "help that persons need in passing from one stage of Christian development to the next."[29] There may be one decisive point, or several points, at which a person "is ready to move out into a greatly increased fruitfulness in his faith."[30] The goal of this whole process of conversion is rebirth.

God as Educator

More by way of summary than of adding any new statement, it can be said that faith belongs only in God. This is a reversal of the earlier twentieth-century confidence in education. Men of Smart's position would say that Christian education can never guarantee results, and that even if it were possible to do so, it would not be permissible to seek control of spiritual growth, which is "a secret, unpredictable matter which cannot be channeled into the official hours of church school or church."[31] The content of the gospel by which man is confronted determines the content of the response in which he appropriates (or rejects) that gospel. "We do not make a person a child of God by telling him that God is his Father. He has been a child of God from the beginning and our words do no more than make him aware of who he is."[32]

"It is God who educates."[33] He uses all the events of life in his education of persons. Thus it might be said that the educator's role is to bring together the person, faced with the mystery of life, and "the Christian revelation of God which alone is the key to the mystery."[34]

Appropriation and Participation

The good news of the gospel and the redemption proclaimed throughout the biblical drama exist as the heritage of the Christian church, "communicated through and by the church" and appropriated as "saving truth" by persons who participate in the ongoing drama of redemption which is the ongoing life of the church.[35] Such is Randolph Crump Miller's view. Learning is always a social process, and "the Gospel of redemption is learned by sharing the redeeming relationships within a community."[36] This community, however, is not an isolated group limited to a particular time and place. Any congregation must be placed within the perspective of all the past, present, and future of God's action in the drama of redemption, a drama re-enacted in the life of that congregation. Moreover, God uses the quality of life in a Christian community to make effectual the power of the gospel "to make new creatures of us."[37] It may be said, therefore, that both God and man have roles in the appropriation of the gospel and in the bringing to pass of "redemption *now.*"

Learning as a Social Process

"The way to become a Christian," Miller says, "is to enter the Church."[38] Why is this so? "Education is a social process," and Christian education occurs when a person participates in the life of two "organisms," the church and the Christian family.[39] From this perspective, Miller deals with the role of experience in learning, the relationship of content and method, and the need for grading in the use of the Bible.

Experience is as important for learning as for revelation because "one discovers the meanings of the Gospel as the Christian life is experienced."[40] At this point Miller acknowledges the validity of John Dewey's thought, indicating, however, that one must *begin* with the Christian truth and then move to an interpretation of experience from that given fact.[41] For the Christian educator, this means many things. It points to the "language of relationships," so closely linked to the concept of experience for Miller. The theology which stands "behind" the curriculum may be interpreted and experienced in terms of relationships before words can be understood.

Thus the great words of biblical theology can be taught from the beginning of childhood. The teacher finds that "the important element is the personal relationships within the class and the relationships that are brought before the class for illumination."[42] There is always the possibility that a class may become "a redemptive cell within the congregation."[43] In a "redemptive cell" a teacher's role is not to contrive experiences which are to be used as illustration for truths to be "learned," but to interpret all experiences of life from the Christian perspective. When a person comes to *see* the truth through having experienced it, he appropriates that truth.

Another implication from the close relating of experience to learning is that thereby worship and evangelism become closely related to education. As Miller says, "It has been discovered that worship is the experience-centered method *par excellence* for educational purposes."[44] This is true when worship is seen as "an activity of one who knows himself to be in the presence of God, to whom the worshiper brings his own difficulties and in the presence of whom he finds solace and power and blessing."[45] Because God is present, not only in worship but in all phases of the teaching of the church, and because Christian education purposes to help bring a person's concerns and the person himself into the presence of God, it may be said that "evangelism and education go hand in hand, and the end of education is conversion to faith in Christ."[46] In fact, there is the double educational and evangelistic aspect of all the functions of the church, and it is through participation in the church that salvation is received.

What is the relationship of method and content to one another and to experience? Method evolves from theology, and there is a "basic relationship between method and subject matter"[47] which appears as truth becomes relevant—and therefore is appropriated —through experience. With this view, Miller's statements that "methods are tools"[48] and that "the problem of method is technical"[49] are a little hard to understand; they do not seem to depict the "organic relation" between content and method for which he contends.[50] On the other hand, it is easy to see the consistency of this "basic relationship" with the values Miller sees in using insight from group dynamics and procedures from the field of group work.[51] It is likewise understandable that he would question whether the "activity" of making a relief map by a fifth grade child would lead the child "farther along the road to becoming a Christian."[52] It might make him "an adequate map maker," but unless there is a relevance of the subject matter used to the child's own religious development, the purpose of Christian education is not accomplished. Nor is it accomplished through indoctrination, or a content approach to learning subject matter. Yet it must be said that Christian education recognizes that the Bible is "worth knowing in itself,"[53] and that factual information must be imparted. But where there is "instruction in factual knowledge" without the atmosphere of Christian love, what occurs "will not be Christian nurture."[54]

In the treatment of the relevance of the Bible to the experiences of various ages, Miller has indicated his recognition of the need for grading or adjusting the Bible story for teaching purposes. Thus "the starting point is the concerns and problems of the learners, both as they see them and as the wise and sensitive teacher leads them to see them."[55] Educators must be concerned about the basic needs and the abilities of persons at every age level, about a person's *"religious readiness,"* or *"the point at*

*which he can reach out and make contact with the meaning of
his world."*[56] This allows for selection and adjustment of Bible
content, but not distortion of the gospel message. What may result is some such generalized strategy of teaching as this:

> For those under twelve, then, the approach to the meaning
> of God will be primarily in terms of actual experiences of
> God at work; for those over twelve, the emphasis will be on
> God as he revealed himself in history and today; while for
> those beyond high school there is the approach through
> philosophical ideas.[57]

The learning which occurs as a social process needs much
skilled guidance combined with devoted planning from a theological perspective if a person is to be helped to develop toward
Christian maturity.

The Drama of Redemption

Learning occurs in ways other than through a social process
centering in experience, according to Miller. Speaking from the
Anglican tradition, he sees that the church itself constantly re-
enacts the drama of redemption through the framework of the
Christian year. Paralleling the teaching program of the church,
where acts of the drama are related to experiences of individuals
and groups, is the preaching ministry, which offers an opportunity for interpretation of the drama.[58] The way in which the
whole life and structure of the church centers around the drama
of redemption increases the probability that biblical facts will
be made alive through experience.

The Redemptive Community

What has already been said about the nature of the church in
relation to revelation and in relation to learning as a social process occurring within a community of persons points to the crucial
center of Miller's understanding of appropriation. "Christian education takes place whenever men respond in faith to the grace
of God channeled through a community of persons, and they are
drawn into a community of the Spirit and participate in the fel-

lowship."[59] *Participation* is a key concept. The three elements pointed out in this statement, faith, grace, and the redemptive community, are the "three elements in religious development."[60] What this approach does is to focus attention on the *koinonia* of the church as "the body of Christ . . . separated from the world and centered in the living Christ as its head."[61]

With Brunner, Miller places emphasis on the fellowship of the church rather than on the church as institution. According to Brunner, the truth which is the love revealed by Jesus Christ lives in the fellowship. According to Miller, the true church is an *"experienced relationship with God and man, and it exists wherever the Holy Spirit rules the hearts of men."*[62] The Word of God does not so much stand over against the church and call it to repentance, which is the view Smart holds, as it lives within the life of the church, constantly seeking to maintain that life against the possible encroachment of the institutional church. It is "an almost impossible demand" that the true church should be experienced within the institutional church or within the "congregation of sinners in need of repentance."[63] Even so, there is a fellowship in this community, an acceptance of one another and a knowledge of self, which means that the ideal is realized at least in part. As members are made anew by the presence of Christ within the community, they receive power to do God's will, to forgive, and to love. Thus they become "a redemptive and sustaining fellowship."[64] When this is said, it must be pointed out specifically that "it is God who does the educating."[65] It is the gift of his grace that he comes to man, revealing himself in such a way that he makes it possible for man to participate in that process. Thus the ever-continuing process of revelation and of appropriation of the redemption offered thereby.

Appropriation and Encounter

Appropriation of the biblical message, for Lewis Sherrill, is a process of changes within the depths of the self in which the self becomes that which God calls it to be within the encounter. The direction of change is determined by the fact that God is present and participant in the Christian community which helps induce, interpret, and sustain the change as it occurs. The Christian community is able to do this, to participate in and guide the changes, to the extent that the language, the materials, and the process of learning open channels of two-way communication. When this is done under the guidance and with the presence of God's Spirit, the "being" of a person who encounters God within the *koinonia* is reborn in a "becoming" which is the response to and the appropriation of revelation.

Encounter Within Community

Psychologically, when even two persons are brought together in a relationship there is set up a dynamic field, a "betweenness" in which the persons involved "do something" to one another. The same thing is true in the more complex web of relationships in a community, which might be defined as *"a body of relationships which affect the becoming of its individual members."*[66] Sherrill points out the fact that in the interaction among persons, destructive as well as constructive elements may be present. It is God's presence in the Christian community, ordained by him as the scene where he constantly confronts man in the redemptive disclosure of himself, which gives a goal and a power for change. This is true whether the *koinonia* be in the church or the household.

The concept of revelation as confrontation implies divine initiative. What, then, about the educator's role? Sherrill says that "the human response to revelation, while it is the direct response of an I to a Thou, is nevertheless open to the kind of guidance which one person may offer to another."[67] Through relationships, the place where change occurs, there is opportunity and responsibility for human participation. To say that man cannot so participate "is a religious form of determinism, the more insidious when it invades the religious community because it has so much to say about giving God the glory."[68]

What is it to say that men influence and participate with one another in the responses which they make to God within the encounter? What men can do, Sherrill says, stands as *"means to the ends sought* in Christian education," and includes such acts as these: "introducing persons to the Christian community, introducing them to the Bible and the Christian heritage, preparing the way for personal response to revelation, participating with them in purposeful action, and counseling with them during periods of crisis."[69]

Whenever and however the call comes to man to move to a higher level of selfhood, of freedom within the Kingdom, of new life in response to God—and the call may come through many media of revelation—that call constitutes a crisis, a confrontation, necessitating an answer. "That is to say, the crisis, which is a time of decision as between advancing into growth or shrinking back from its perils, is a time when God confronts the human creature."[70] Whether confrontation occurs through traumatic crises or through minor decisions day by day, whether experience is recognized instantaneously or in retrospect as confrontation by Deity, the fact remains that it is only because of the experience of encounter where Christians support one another in their response that change is possible.

Communication

An understanding of man's role in appropriation of the biblical message seems to center primarily around the concept of communication, for "the fact of God's presence with man needs to be constantly interpreted to persons of all ages and stages of life so that they may perceive it."[71] Unless they *do* perceive it, there has been no real communication. Out of a much fuller treatment, three aspects of Sherrill's thought concerning this subject have been selected as being most relevant to the question at hand. They are the language, the materials, and the process of communication.

In the first place, communication cannot occur unless there is a *language* which serves as a common starting point, a language which means essentially the same thing to different people. That language is to be found primarily in the Bible, "the mother tongue of the Christian community."[72] Persons and events in Bible history must be known, for they are "the indispensable stuff out of which the themes are built."[73] Meaning is rooted in these particulars, although meaning transcends them. What this signifies is that "it is not only permissible, it is necessary to include instruction in Biblical content as part of the curriculum."[74] Men cannot affirm biblical history as "their" history until they know and can communicate with one another about it; only then can that history become living and revelatory.

A part of the language of the Bible is its symbols, and these are a chief factor in making communication possible. The emphasis Sherrill places on symbols reminds one of Tillich. Although both signs and symbols are means of communication, Sherrill uses the term "sign" as the more inclusive, and distinguishes among arbitrary signs, icons, and symbols. Symbols are essential for communication regarding the encounter with God. Whether one refers to an object, as "blood" or "altar," or to events, as the establishing of the covenant, the whole range of biblical symbols is both *"the language through which God discloses himself to man"* and *"the basic vocabulary of communication within the Christian community."*[75] What a symbol represents cannot be communicated in nonsymbolic language nor grasped by the ordinary use of the senses. It is so organically and inwardly related to that which it represents and to the community assigning meaning to it that it may be said both to participate in the reality to which it refers and to be capable of communicating power.

There is a sense, then, in which the Christian community cannot perpetuate its heritage or itself, cannot evoke change through communication, apart from the events, the words, the symbols of the Bible. There is another language of communication, the nonverbal language of relationships. "The Bible itself shows that the highest form of communication is not by means of precise verbalism, but is carried on by means of what passes between persons in personal encounter."[76] The ideal situation for communication existed in the Jewish family, Sherrill says, where relationships, experiences, and rituals were given content by verbalized interpretations, and where questions of the young forced the more mature to reach out for deeper levels of meaning. This education has a "touch of genius" in it, and shows how different "languages" may re-enforce each other in such a way that real learning is made possible.[77]

The language of communication is drawn from the *materials* used for teaching purposes. "The *materials* of learning are matters originally outside the self, presented to the self, and employed by responsible persons as means to ends. The ends for which the materials are employed are changes in persons."[78] A curriculum cannot be completely planned; the events in lives of group members may become "materials" for learning as they are "thrown into an already dynamic situation" and precipitate "fresh interaction between the persons."[79] In the planned curriculum, however, there is an "immense range of materials to draw upon."[80] But the biblical materials are basic, not only because they provide the language of communication and make remembrance possible, but also because they describe a "continuing confrontation" and "can awaken and foster man's continuing perception of this continuing divine confrontation, and can guide his continuing response to it."[81]

The important question, with reference to communication, has to do with the use of the Bible with children, for the Bible is an adult book. Sherrill states that "each theme of revelation probably is relevant ultimately to every age in the life span," and that a theme "can be communicated non-verbally from the earliest days of life," then communicated both "verbally and symbolically as age advances."[82] Work needs to be done on adapting biblical materials so that themes most appropriate to varying ages may be emphasized, and so that there may be "progression in the development of a theme from one age group to another," as well as "progression in the use of symbols."[83] Because what is communicated nonverbally is so basic, it is important to begin with adults in "the strategy of education planning."[84]

The *process* of communication has to do with interaction among persons. Such interaction sets up a two-way current in which there is both an educing and an imparting. "Education is the leading out, the leading forth or calling forth of one self by another self. Impartation is the giving forth of at least a part of one self who is in communication with another."[85] Of course eduction may degenerate into manipulation, and impartation into transmitting of materials as a substitute for the offer of oneself, but when the two occur without distortion in the Christian community, then a genuine two-way communication between selves is set up. This is in direct contrast to one-way communication, in which communication is by pressure, and is an effort to "do something" to people or to "put something across."[86] On the other hand, two-way communication "flows in both directions," in a mutuality in which "each gives forth something of himself."[87] This is the I-Thou relationship made familiar by Martin Buber.

What are the implications for methodology of Christian education if communication is considered primarily as the process of interaction among selves? One implication is that there is no one "best" method. A method may be chosen on the basis of whether it facilitates two-way communication and of the kind of interaction which it sets up between persons.[88] Method has something to do with what happens to persons. It sets up interaction which may be either spiritual and healing, or demonic and damaging to selves.

Another implication is that different methods do not have to be developed for using the Bible, so long as the center of concern is with communication between selves. There is value, however, in finding those methods which best permit nonverbal as well as verbal communication, which help people "stand inside the Bible and participate with its people in their encounter with God,"[89] and which use biblical materials as a "means for changing the perception of the meaning in the total configuration of things which life presents."[90] Such methods will employ symbolic communication, and will call forth doubt as well as faith, using feelings of ambivalence as a means of growth. Such methods are possible only when there is a deep and genuine communication between selves. *That* kind of communication, to the degree in which persons who participate have experienced the love of God, is itself Christian education. It is the profoundest kind of communication; "the interaction which takes place is nothing less than the interpenetration of selves into one another."[91] Such communication becomes communion, and is in itself "an ultimate good."[92]

Being and Becoming

A person is always both a "being" and a "becoming." Christian education, which is concerned with changes in the depths of the self, is possible because a person *can* "become," because learning is a dynamic process of tension, interaction, and change in which human beings influence and participate with one another in change.[93] The consideration of communication has indicated the nature of that influence and participation.

As to what happens within a person during the process of learning or becoming, many descriptions may be offered. In Jewish education, people were said to learn the Torah by such things as "discernment of heart, by pureness, by discussion with associates, by Scripture, by being loved, by loving God, by loving mankind, and so on."[94] Or again, it could be learned by "being obeyed."[95] In the New Testament, the teachings of Jesus had "peculiarly penetrating quality" which necessitated "relentless probing for first things in living."

> The meaning for education is readily seen. When persons in any age not merely receive the objective facts of his life, teaching, death, and resurrection, but whenever they also commence to "work over" the meaning, pondering it, absorbing it into the deepest recesses of thinking, new life begins to break forth because new meaning has begun to break in.[96]

In addition to these and other biblical references to learning, Sherrill turns to the field of psychology and selects two from the various approaches to learning as being most appropriate to Christian education. From the field of Gestalt psychology comes the recognition that a self responds as a total self to a whole field; a group of persons constitutes a "power field." Also from Gestalt psychology comes "the principle of insight," by which a person is held to *"perceive meaning"* because "the parts in the total field stand in a relationship to one another which he is capable of mentally grasping."[97] Such perception may come after times of frustration because no meaning is apparent; the shifting in the configuration or in perception leads to "a sense of meaning perceived" and may "cause power to be released or redirected."[98]

Depth psychology, with its analytical methods of understanding the unconscious, also points up the importance of relationships as playing a role in the changes that take place in persons. But "in religious thought 'relationships' are conceived in a cosmic frame of reference. Thus when it is said that the deeper changes take place in relationships, the statement refers not only to relationships with other human beings, but also to the relationship with God."[99] And what happens in the relationship with God is that a new self is called into being by love, a love which is foreshadowed by and communicated through human love, imperfect though that human love may be.[100]

It may be said, then, that to be and to become a Christian is a "struggle of the soul," a life which is a pilgrimage. The changes which occur, Sherrill says, cannot always be explained by the terms "growth" or "conversion." Often a person passes through many "revolutionary changes in the self during the course of a lifetime," changes which are "radical shifts in the total pattern which life presents."[101] The shifts result from a lifelong process of confrontation of man by God, often through "circumstances of the common life" as "the form in which God comes again into our little part of human history, coming thus to our senses, confronting us, calling on us for the response of faith to the end that we may 'enter in' a little further."[102]

When man does "enter in" through faith, what happens is that he takes hold of salvation, of the "substance" of reality, and begins to live "by it and in it."[103] He loves in response to love, and so is reborn of the Spirit. This is the appropriation of revelation.

It can be experienced, it can be witnessed to in the worshiping community which is itself the matrix within which the members achieve their destiny, and it can be accepted with awe and thanksgiving as the impartation of God's grace.

Summary

One word which might be chosen to designate the very essence of appropriation of the biblical message as understood by all those writers considered here is *response*. It is a word which signifies God's initiative, yet allows room for human channels of communication. It is a word of theological import and yet permits variation in theories of learning. Iris Cully specifically defines appropriation as "man's response to revelation."[104] In so doing, she is reflecting a growing agreement among Christian educators.

But it is difficult to generalize about Christian educators' understanding of the nature of appropriation, because great numbers of persons have produced books which bear directly on this area. Authors deal primarily with methods or psychological and sociological analyses, and it is often hard to determine what theory undergirds their approaches. However, it seems increasingly true that even the most practically oriented books, written specifically to help a teacher carry out his responsibilities, are taking into account many of the theoretical and theological insights mentioned here. Ethel L. Smither's *Children and the Bible* (1960) and Robert E. Koenig's *The Use of the Bible with Adults* (1959), although differing in basic theory at many points, are two examples of this fact. Then, too, there are a number of writers who, particularly with respect to this area of appropriation, seem to hold on to an old stream of educational philosophy upon which some of the newer theological concepts have been grafted without the two becoming fully merged.

It seems safe to generalize further and say that there is a steady movement toward recognizing both the experiential and factual elements in learning, toward viewing the Christian communities of home and church as the matrix for Christian education, and toward finding appropriate ways to place the Bible in its true role as witness to revelation. Such writers as Vieth, Wyckoff, and Grimes, as well as Cully, move in this direction. Langford is close to Smart, Howe to Miller, and Johnson to Sherrill in particular emphases made by these men.

Comparison is difficult for an area where insights from many disciplines of thought are brought together and utilized in the formulation of theories and principles underlying communication as it relates to the teaching ministry of the church. Such comparison as is attempted here proceeds from a consideration of three concepts: relationship, confrontation, and learning.

Relationship is a key word for communication. The emphasis of Miller and Sherrill on the fact that the biblical message of salvation is to be understood, witnessed to, and communicated primarily through human and divine-human relationships may owe much to Brunner's concept of encounter, to his and Farmer's biblical personalism, or to the "I-Thou" emphasis of the Jewish theologian Martin Buber. Particularly for Sherrill, there is the possibility of influence from the fields of Gestalt and depth psychology, stressing the importance of relationships. Miller draws from the field of group dynamics. Both men hold that human love may bear within it a quality which mediates divine love. For Miller, it is almost as though the experience of being related to one another and to God becomes the medium through which salvation is appropriated. For Sherrill, emphasis is on the spiritual and demonic forces inherent in the structure of relationships; change occurs according to the nature of the forces brought to bear upon persons. For Smart, as well as Barth, the form of relationships among men is more an outcome of their relationship with God than a channel for receiving the love of God.

Confrontation as related to education implies that only as God reveals himself is salvation offered or may it be received. It is to God's confrontation that response takes place. That to which response is made is emphasized more by Smart; the act of responding more by Miller. Although Sherrill refers often to the concept of confrontation, the term "encounter" was purposely used in relation to appropriation, in that it points up more the participation of men with one another in their reception of and response to revelation. Smart's idea of confrontation is more in terms of Truth bearing its own authority and winning its own mode of human reception. Sherrill seems to see confrontation as coming more through experiential crises of life in which God as Person is perceived to be in a relationship with man which offers power to overcome those crises and to be redeemed. Miller is closer to Sherrill, though his terminology differs. With him, as with Temple, the subjective experience of perceiving meaning in God's action completes that action and constitutes revelation. He can thereby assign to both experience and reason a role in "learning."

What does the fact of confrontation have to do with the role of reason in appropriation? Christian educators seem agreed that facts, the biblical heritage, must be taught. This necessitates the use of reason. So does the effort to perceive meaning in the heritage, and in present experience. Smart has little further to say, but he speaks of "delving" into meaning, of "instructing the conscience." Sherrill has little to say directly, either, although he speaks of "natural processes" being "transformed" by revelation. More thinking about this subject is needed by Christian educators, particularly in the light of possible contributions from Brunner (for whom reason may be a channel for the appropriation of revelation), Tillich (for whom reason is "fulfilled" by revelation, after preparing the way for its reception), and Niebuhr (for whom reason is "transformed" by revelation). Miller deals with the matter more directly than either Smart or Sherrill and attaches more importance to the role of reason than they seem to do.

Learning, it seems, is being redefined in terms of its relation to revelation. God's purpose in self-revelation is man's redemption. This means that learning has to do with the rebirth of the self. Man cannot control that kind of change by knowing the "laws of learning" or by manipulation or by focusing on conduct. Therefore his role is more accurately described by such phrases as being, witnessing, interpreting, participating, repenting, using methods which open channels of communication between selves, instructing in biblical facts for the sake of their message. Most theologians and educators would agree that these are legitimate activities of man, but that always it is God who makes possible the learning, the changes in the self, which are appropriation of the message of the Bible.

There is a demonstrable consistency of thought in each writer's theological perspective and his understanding of the appropriation of the biblical message. As one moves from the more theoretical to the more practical consideration of appropriation, he is faced with such questions as the structure of the curriculum, and the organization of subject matter for teaching. Although no one writer has developed a complete curriculum plan himself, and therefore a further check on consistency cannot be made, it is interesting to observe that there are curriculum patterns now in existence which seem at least partially to give form to the philosophy which has been presented.

The statement cannot be documented here, but it seems safe to say that the Christian Faith and Life curriculum of the United Presbyterian Church illustrates the practical implications of James Smart's position and the Seabury Series of the Episcopal Church does the same thing for Randolph Crump Miller's position. Perhaps this is true not so much because the philosophical position has been previously conceived and then applied as because the philosophy has been "hammered out" while both these men were involved in working out the two pioneering curriculum developments of this current period. Smart served as first editor for Faith and Life materials, and Miller served in advisory capacity for the Seabury materials. Outside these two patterns there is still the continuation of the older traditions, both of liberalism and of fundamentalism. No one pattern can be pointed to in connection with Lewis Sherrill. He served as consultant for the restudy of educational philosophy and curriculum in his own denomination, the Presbyterian Church in the United States (Southern).[105] That study is still under way; as a new curriculum emerges there, it will be instructive to compare it with the thought of Sherrill. Generally speaking, there is great activity in the field of curriculum development during these days, and the creative potential in the situation indicates an openness to the resurgence of interest in philosophy of Christian education.

VII Consensus and Divergence

Whatever else may be said, the role of the Bible in contemporary Christian education in America is decidedly different from that which it played during the first three or four decades of this century. This conclusion is based upon cumulative evidence gained from tracing the process by which certain definable and accepted patterns of thought concerning the Bible were disrupted and passed through a period of conflict and transition toward a reformulation in different forms. The general trend of thought of the educational leaders today marks the new role as distinctive and in contrast to the old. Yet many of the constituent elements of the old are to be found in the new, seen now in different combinations, and viewed from a changed perspective giving the elements a different orientation. The new is thus continuous with the old.

It is agreed today that the Bible is not a textbook or reference book or code of conduct. It is a book which is generically different from other books. One turns to it with an attitude of serious expectancy; one speaks of its message with a note of imperative urgency; one becomes aware of its soteriological implications as he struggles to find within the record meaning which can become a medium for continuing revelation. This attitude creates a pervasive atmosphere which is different from the kind of permissiveness prevailing when the Bible was held in "high regard."

The newer view gives to the Bible an authority which does not limit but becomes a source of power, an authority which becomes actualized as men respond to and thereby appropriate the biblical message. No symbol, no institution, can play quite the same role as the Bible. Its words are the most reliable witness to and channel for God's revelation. Thus, whether one speaks of revelation or redemption, of theology or ethics, of authority or experience, of Christian truth or relevance, he cannot escape reference to the Bible. The role it plays in Christian education today focuses attention again upon its centrality in communication of the faith.

Earlier it was suggested that the average church member might question the meaning of such statements as God "speaks" to and "meets" a person in the Bible, or through the Bible one may come to participate in the "drama of redemption." Explanation of the meaning constitutes what might be considered agreement in the understanding of the Bible which is becoming increasingly clear in Christian education, and which is in basic accord with theological and biblical scholarship.

It is almost immediately apparent that these words and phrases do not focus attention on infallible words or propositional truths to be mastered. Nor do they suggest the possibility of a casual reference to the Bible when need arises. What is actually meant is not so readily manifest. Uninterpreted, the terms may seem to assign to the Bible almost a magic power to effect immediate awareness of God and a personal relationship with him, thus developing false expectancies and misdirected efforts on the part of the teacher or reader of the Bible. What can be said in answer to the question of meaning is quite different.

To say that the Bible "speaks" to a person may mean that it brings new insight to him, that it illumines his problems, that it enables him to see new meaning in life viewed as a whole. But any book, event, person, or thing could "speak" to a person in such a way. The important thing is not *that* the Bible speaks, but *what it says*. Its witness to the fact and the meaning of God's actions in history makes possible for man the factual and experiential knowledge that God's love reaches out to him in a judgment and a healing that is salvation. When man perceives that fact, the Bible "speaks" to him directly at the deepest level of existence.

More than that, the Bible becomes the instrument for drawing man into a relationship with God; man "meets" God; the words become the Word, God's self-revelation. Man's response to this confrontation is an entering into a covenant relationship with God which is the basis for all his decisions, which is the matrix within which he becomes that which God calls him to be, and which is, indeed, a participation in the drama of redemption. The Bible thus becomes the witness to and the channel for God's revelation of himself.

This brief explanation, which might offer to the layman some insight into terms used so frequently as almost to have become catchwords, includes within it the general agreement in the current understanding of the Bible. More analytically, it might be said that the consensus as to the role of the Bible in Christian education covers four areas.

First, there seems to be unanimity as to the understanding of the purpose of the biblical witness: to hold out to man the offer of salvation. This salvation is both ultimate and immediate, both eschatological and to be realized in the specifics of daily human action. To the degree to which men respond in faith and obedience to the biblical witness they demonstrate its relevance and receive the salvation it offers. To that degree, its purpose is accomplished. Whatever use is made of the Bible in Christian education must be in keeping with this understanding.

Second, the nature of the biblical witness may be understood as *Heilsgeschichte*, a history of salvation. It unites Old and New Testaments in one message of salvation, culminating in the life, death, and resurrection of Jesus Christ. Whatever differences may exist as to how the biblical witness is to be formulated, there is agreement on the message it bears and on the fact that it is an interpreted account of God's actions in history for man's salvation. There is a divine purposiveness in providing a concrete biblical form that challenges the efforts of man and the church. Engaging in dialogue with the Bible may lead to a perception and experience of God's continuing work of revelation and reconciliation.

Third, the Bible cannot be understood apart from the fact of revelation. This is clear from what has been said about the nature and purpose of the biblical witness, in spite of differences that may exist concerning the doctrine of revelation. It is God's action in revelation which is redemptive, not the Bible. And revelation is not to be equated with the words of the Bible. It is something that happens, a dynamic, not something that can be "taught." Yet it is true that man can know neither the fact of God's action nor its meaning apart from the Bible, which is therefore organically involved in the fact of revelation. Even those who recognize a general revelation acknowledge the prior necessity of the special biblical revelation. Because of this, the Bible is generally recognized as the supreme, if not the sole, authority. This is no stultifying human authority, for the Bible mediates the authority of God. The centrality of the Bible in the teaching program of the church may be ascribed to the nature of its authority and its relationship with revelation.

Fourth, a curriculum which might be designated *gospel-centered* seems to be most consistent with the understanding of the Bible expressed here. It is at this point that the "new" in Christian education presents itself most decisively. Such a curriculum centers more on the message and purpose of the Bible than on the exact text. It recognizes the value of higher criticism but assigns greater importance to the theological interpretation of events recorded in the Bible, finding meaning and relevance for life today through this interpretation. It is built neither around the Bible as subject matter nor around the "felt needs" and problems of persons as the key to what is to be taught.

The purpose of teaching is the communication of the gospel, and this involves both direct study *about* the gospel as revealed in the Bible, and the experience of the meaning of the gospel within the context of the worshiping Christian community of church and home. The direct teaching utilizes the most effective known educational methods as evaluated theologically and ethically, and takes advantage of the insights of sociology and psychology in its relating of the Bible's message to persons individually and in groups. The fact and the possibility of non-verbal teaching stand as judgment and as challenge to the church, which cannot control the communication of its faith but which influences that communication through what it teaches, how it teaches, what it is. In the final analysis the purpose of teaching is realized through the work of the Holy Spirit. A person appropriates the gospel through his response to it within *koinonia;* he comes to know its reality and power within the covenant relationship, where he is enabled to know the truth by doing it.

In the light of the added emphasis on meaning and message, and on God's role in the appropriation of revelation, it is important to note that there is no negation of the importance of teaching facts, nor of the role of reason and experience in learning, contrary to fears that have been voiced. There is general agreement in the educational writings that meaning transcends historical events but is rooted in those events; therefore events must be taught as facts if meaning is to be perceived. Or, as Richard Niebuhr says, there is no inner history apart from outer history, and this outer history must be known if persons are to identify themselves with and participate in the continuous inner history of the Judaic-Christian community. There is a variation in emphasis and understanding of the implications of such a statement in the writings studied, but there would be little disagreement with the theory it expresses.

Reason and experience have to do primarily, although not exclusively, with the interpretation and appropriation of revelation. And there would probably be agreement among theologians and educators that, although revelation is confrontation by the living God, although it is something that "happens," it is not "pure immediacy." It has a content that is communicable. If this were not so, there would be no occasion for the educational ministry of the church. Niebuhr summarizes the matter again. He suggests that the traditions, the concepts, and the ideas man has acquired as the response of other persons to revelation, the meaning perceived in experience—all these become a "content" to be brought under the bright light of God's self-disclosure and there continuously transformed by the "reasoning heart." Revelation calls for the use of reason and is appropriated within experience.

What all this says to the subject of investigation is that the Bible has to do with both the content and the purpose of Christian education. More than that, if the biblical message is to be appropriated, it must be placed in a setting which supports it and gives it meaning. Therefore, curriculum must be interpreted in terms comprehensive enough to include the whole faith and life of the Christian community. The term "gospel-centered curriculum" indicates something of the current understanding of the approach involved if the Bible is really to be taught and learned in accordance with what it is.

Within this general background of agreement there are divergences of theory and implications for practice, clustering mostly around two poles of thought concerning the Bible and its role in Christian education. The first pole emphasizes primarily the *content* of the Bible. By this is not meant subject matter, but the dynamic inherent within the biblical message. The approach is essentially a continuation of the Reformation emphasis on the Bible as the Word of God. It recognizes the fact that the words of the Bible are the form bearing God's self-revelation, and that content cannot be approached, perceived, or communicated apart from form. The miracle, as Karl Barth sees it, is that God in his freedom gives himself to be known through human words, but is never limited by them; the words, in turn, remain human words, and yet are a unity with the content they bear. The educational implication of this view is a greater emphasis on subject matter than in other schools of thought, but the emphasis is to be interpreted in terms of the relationship between form and content, which suggests that study of subject matter may eventuate in confrontation.

What this suggests is that the divine content has within it the power to effect transformation of persons. The work of the Holy Spirit in making possible the reception of the biblical message is an organic aspect of God's revelatory activity, inextricably related to the biblical form. The educator can prepare the way by making known the language and heritage of the Christian community, can interpret, can encourage people to witness to one another concerning their faith, but his essential task is to bring persons into a relationship with the biblical message, which can do its own work. One does not have to determine what a person should be like. The new life which is his with his faith-response to God is a "becoming," the fulfillment of his calling. It is an expression of what a person believes to be true. Therefore—and this again is consistent with the emphasis on content—doctrine is of great importance. This is the Calvinistic tradition.

The second pole of thought emphasizes primarily the *process* by which God has revealed himself through the Bible, the same process by which he continues to make himself known today. The Bible is a record of God's "mighty acts" along with the interpretation of God's purpose in those acts. It is therefore a record of revelation, for, as Temple, Brunner, Miller, and Sherrill, among others, would say, revelation occurs when there is the event of God's action and the perception of the meaning in event. But the point of special significance is that the dramatic movement of God's action in history continues in the present, and that men today are unable to interpret history or their own lives except by reference to the meaning revealed in the Bible. When persons perceive the relevance of that meaning to their own lives, they recognize that they are experiencing the very essence of the truth recorded in the Bible. The relationship God had with his people in the Bible is the same relationship he has with persons today who respond to him. It is an "I-Thou" relationship which could not be known apart from the biblical revelation, and it is within the reality of continuing revelation that biblical truth is understood and appropriated.

There is another key emphasis within this second area of thought. Men come to know the reality to which doctrine points through their relationship with persons who are being transformed by it. This is the language of relationships, which is as decisive a language as that of words and which is, indeed, necessary to give meaning to the great words of the Christian tradition.

The believing community, the *koinonia* within which God is present, is redemptive. In that community, truth is translated into life and experienced there. What this means for the educator is that he will be concerned with the process through which experience is illumined by reference to the Bible, and through which man's deepest religious needs are met by the appropriation of the biblical faith when one comes to know the truth by experiencing it.

These two approaches are not set forth as categorically different. A general area of agreement has already been indicated, and what is intended here is to point to major differences in emphasis. The first approach is more concerned with content, with the Word of God; the second with process, with the Acts of God. The first gives more attention to God's purpose; the second, to man's need and experience. Whereas the Bible has more a commanding authority for the first group and serves to confront man, it has more a teaching authority for the second group and serves as resource. Appropriation is to be understood more in terms of response for the first group, of participation for the second group.

Insofar as the historical development of the curriculum of Christian education is concerned, the first approach has some affinities with the "Bible-centered curriculum" and with the fundamentalistic position in its devotion to the Bible. But whereas the "content" pole of thought recaptures much of the Reformation spirit, the fundamentalistic position perpetuates the aberration of Protestant scholasticism. Moreover, the distinction must be made between the content emphasis of one and the subject matter emphasis of the other, for the two are not the same.

The second approach stands more in the stream of the liberal tradition and the "experience-centered curriculum" as developed by Coe and Bower. But whereas the "process" pole of thought radically modifies the older position through its reformulation of the doctrine of revelation and its bringing the note of depth into the concept of experience, the unreconstructed experience-centered curriculum flounders in its lack of any clear understanding of itself. Other comparisons might be made, but trends are evident from what has been said.

How does Christian education today orient itself with reference to these two poles of thought? From the writings studied, it is possible to delineate three patterns with respect to the role of the Bible—patterns operative within the central core of American Protestantism, and not including the fundamentalistic and humanistic views of the Bible, outside and at opposite ends of the continuum running from one pole of thought to the other.

The first pattern, centering around Smart's position, is to be closely identified with the "content" pole, carrying on the Reformation tradition. Both Sherrill and Miller are closer to the "process" emphasis, but it is Miller who is the key representative of that position, carrying on the Anglican tradition and the irenic spirit of Temple's theology. It is more exact to view Sherrill as representative of a third pattern, combining emphases from the two poles of thought, not eclectically but in a synthesis. Or perhaps it would be better to say that the pattern centering in his thought represents something of a dialogue between the theology of relationships and the theology of confrontation. The resultant position in turn interacts with educational philosophy and depth psychology to move toward an understanding and use of the Bible which mediates between the two poles of thought described here.

These three positions do not represent "schools of thought." Yet, although many writers today resist categorizing, it would be possible to interpret most theoretical writing by reference to the three positions delineated here.

Both the *content* and the *process* approaches have potentialities for moving beyond a "Bible-centered," "pupil-centered," or "experienced-centered" view of curriculum to a "gospel-centered" approach. This may represent a new point of relative stability to which Christian educators have moved in their thinking. Even so, although many trends seem to have converged during these times to produce this stability, there is still enough evidence of disagreement, enough difference in major emphases, even in the three positions described here, to provoke further thought. And the conflicts become rampant when effort is made to develop what is in fact and not only in theory a "gospel-centered" curriculum.

VIII Toward a Point of View

To trace the changes in the role of the Bible is, in a sense, to elucidate developments in philosophy of Christian education. As that role has undergone radical change in recent years, it has come to have a profound influence on Christian education itself. Standing both within and over against the process of Christian education, the Bible has become a dynamic norm by which contemporary Christian education is enabled to understand itself and to be continuously transformed to fulfill more effectively its function in the Christian community. Because this is true, at least two insights have emerged which seem relevant to the possible direction of future developments.

In the first place, that kind of Christian education in which the Bible will continue to be a determinative influence will not understand itself to be an autonomous discipline. It is a mediating discipline, an area in which conversation may be carried on among various and numerous disciplines of thought, with the goal of merging together those factors most relevant to Christian communication and transforming them into forms suitable to the content to be communicated.

First one field of thought and then another seems to exercise a dominant influence in Christian education. With George Albert Coe it was psychology of religion. With William C. Bower it was educational philosophy. More recently, with James Smart and Randolph Crump Miller, it has been theology—the area of thought still making the greatest impact on Christian education. Other persons, like Paul H. Vieth and Lewis J. Sherrill, have reached out from within Christian education to draw in and util-

ize thought from other fields. It seems logical to assume that
Christian education has no independent status, no unique and
continuing core of thought to which it gives attention. It is to be
defined in terms of its function of communication, and the content
which is to be communicated, by which it is enabled to screen
and accept influences from the many disciplines clamoring for
attention.

In the second place, the "gospel-centered curriculum," which
gives much promise for assigning to the Bible its proper role,
needs thoughtful consideration as the task of Christian education
is defined more precisely. In these days when the Christian education program assumes such massive proportions as to be un-
wieldly, its function is blurred, and man is encouraged to live out
his vocation in church activities rather than in the world.

Perhaps some definition relating the concept of curriculum
more directly to the doctrine of revelation would be helpful.
That which distinguishes the curriculum of Christian education
from all other curricula is the fact of revelation. It is determinative of the purpose and the content of the curriculum and becomes the point of reference by which insights from all other
disciplines are utilized. Such a definition is proposed here with
the belief that, developed consistently, it would be a way of
limiting and focusing the church's responsibility in Christian
education. This is the suggestion: *the curriculum of Christian
education designates those occasions in which the church witnesses
to the fact of revelation, interprets its meaning, endeavors to
understand its contemporary relevance, and responds to it in
worship and commitment.*

Whether such a definition would stand up under testing remains to be seen. But there is need for a determinative principle
by which curriculum can be *planned.* There is no need in Christian education to contrive situations in which Christian teaching
may be "practiced," or to introduce endless projects which are no
more than busywork. There is no need to duplicate the efforts
of other agencies, or to become competitors with other churches,
envious of the complexity of their programs.

What is essential is to hold out to man God's offer of salvation in such a way that man may perceive its meaning, and to support him in his response to that offer. This would mean, in the first place, that the church is responsible for enabling man to hear of the historical events witnessed to and interpreted in the Bible, as well as of the witness of members of the Christian community throughout history and in the present to the meaning in God's action. This is witnessing to and interpreting the fact of revelation.

In the second place, if the church corporately and Christians individually really minister to the world, living out in the world their response to God's redemption, occasions must be provided in which direct consideration is given to social problems in terms of Christian obligation. This is the effort to understand the contemporary relevance of revelation. It may call for much study and analysis of subjects other than biblical. Decision regarding responsibility in these times must be in terms of both situation and Christian imperative. This Christian imperative springs from the total biblical message, not from a single verse.

Thus the church provides a point of beginning and of return. It offers a perspective touching every area of life, but does not control every area. It nourishes its members, binding them together through worship and supporting them in their deepening commitment.

These planned occasions, centering around the essential task of Christian education and forming the basis for all aspects of the church's mission, constitute a way in which men may seek to understand God's continuing action in relating himself to his people. When through these occasions men come to participate in the life of the people of God, that participation becomes the experience within which the salvation offered through revelation is appropriated as new life.

What about the role of the Bible in the future? It may be noted that in spite of all the vitality of the "new" philosophy of Christian education, there is little evidence of confidence or finality when educators speak of the appropriation of the biblical message. Perhaps this is essential to a teaching ministry that must always seek to be flexible in relationship to the forms through which it must communicate to changing culture. There are no divine directives pointed to the specifics of the professional tasks of education. These must be worked out, with "painful thought," over and over, in ever-changing situations. But even so, it will never be possible to speak with assurance about how a transcendent Christianity is to be communicated. What is suggested here, therefore, is more a dialogue than a position; it is only movement toward a point of view.

The Word and the Record

There are significant implications for Christian education in a view of the Bible which propounds its divine-human nature, with the two elements always in tension and in unity, with the absolute communicated through but not identified with the relative, with the divine Word borne by and participating in the human record which is distinct from it. That is to say, man cannot seem to bypass the relative form, the human record, in direct access to the divine, but in the act of grappling with the concrete human form, one may be preparing the way to be grasped by, or brought into encounter with, God himself. Somehow the nature of the biblical witness seems to be such that a person must become involved himself, must put forth effort to understand, if he is to appropriate the biblical faith.

Perhaps this is why the so-called rediscovery of the Bible is of such importance for Christian education. Yet it may be more accurate to say that the biblical message, rather than the Bible, has been rediscovered. Herein may lie the faint hint of a danger signal. Like the Reformers, seminal thinkers of this century have been encountered by the Bible and have offered an explication of its message. The Reformers' message, however, developed into a system to which people turned instead of to the Bible, so that the movement lost its vitality. There is always the possibility of a repetition of that development. Certainly on every hand there are directions to study the Bible, but in the Reformed tradition today there is easily the possibility that more emphasis may be placed on the communication of previous correct interpretation than on direct Bible study. Or in the "process" approach there is the possibility of overlooking the Bible in the search for the meaning in experience. Christian education theorists need to give more attention to principles of interpretation and to ways persons and groups may delve into the biblical message themselves in the effort to interpret it.

The "Word and record" nature of the Bible calls for the efforts of a person to offer his interpretation of what he finds, checked by the interpretations of others. There is a sense in which a person cannot appropriate faith unless he can articulate its meaning. This may be one of the reasons why participation is desirable in learning situations, and why insights or discoveries become both possessions and determining forces in a person's life more definitely when they are verbalized. The concern here is with the nature of learning as well as with the nature of the Bible, and at this point is directed more to youth and adults than to children.

The emphasis on confrontation by the Word through the study of the record has already rendered a great service in its recapturing of the biblical concept of a personal meeting between man and God in which God himself is revealed. But here again there is the possibility of misinterpretation. Teachers may feel frustrated or guilty if they do not see evidence of confrontation at every session of the Sunday church school. Perhaps this calls for a more precise theoretical clarification of the function of Christian education in relationship to confrontation. When such clarification comes, both theorists and laymen must recognize the role of education in providing a basic knowledge of the Bible, or what Clarence Tucker Craig calls the factual presentation of the record of revelation. There need be no apology for the presentation of the bases of the gospel faith, although information is never presented solely for the sake of information.

The teacher's hope and expectation is that there will be occasions in which information about the Bible, the subject matter discussed in classes, will be caught up and transformed into the meaning possible only when one is aware of God's self-communication. Such an encounter cannot be contrived by the teacher; it is the work of the Holy Spirit and affects the teacher as much as the student. And confrontation need not occur within the walls of the church building, although that to which the church witnesses is responsible for confrontation.

But, as has already been stated, encounter is not to be defined solely in terms of a quasi-mystical or emotional experience. Kierkegaard relates emotion to reason, experience to communication, and both to appropriation of revelation in a way remarkable for one who has often been accused of being an irrationalist. As he says, emotion which is Christian is to be expressed and communicated in terms of Christian concepts; it is no more than "twaddle" to express emotion without strict discipline in the language of those concepts. "For a Christian awakening what is required, on the one hand, is being grasped in a Christian sense and, on the other hand, conceptual and terminological firmness and definiteness."[1] Statements such as these, with their many implications for Christian education in relation to the experiential and intellectual factors in faith and to the "Word and record" nature of the Bible, point to other related concerns.

The Subjective and the Objective

Educators agreeing about the meaning of revelation expressly recognize the interdependence of objective and subjective factors in revelation, and expressly state that the biblical witness to revelation accomplishes its purpose only when man perceives, subjectively, the meaning of revelation for his own existence. Nevertheless, there is often discernible in Christian education a tendency to emphasize one factor as over against the other. Stress on the objective factor seems to be accompanied by an overemphasis on the intellectual aspect of faith; stress on the subjective factor, by overemphasis on the experiential. In all writings studied, both factors are recognized, so it is important to note the term "overemphasis."

More specifically, in that area of thought emphasizing the

"content" of the Bible, attention is centered on the objective fact of revelation. This has the advantage of leading a person to turn attention away from himself toward God, to direct his efforts toward understanding the meaning in God's actions, to come to self-knowledge in the light of his knowledge of God and to be changed in conformity with that knowledge.

On the other hand, overemphasis here has at least two undesirable results. It seems to have led to the conviction in certain educators and theologians that their interpretation of the meaning in God's action is authoritative, and, with their belief that "vagueness is safe but ineffectual," they have moved toward a dogmatism that is the exact opposite of vagueness. Even Karl Barth expresses the fear "that all of us are on the point of becoming far too positive."[2] What happens is that educators recognize the role doubt has to play in enabling persons to become involved in the content which can resolve their doubt and change them, but the tone of assurance closes the door to the possibility of the ambivalent feelings educators verbally encourage. A second undesirable result is the neglect of the nonverbal aspect of communication, of the "relationship theology" which engenders awareness of persons and their need to find what truth means for *them.*

The emphasis on the "process" by which God revealed and continues to reveal himself seems to center on the subjective factor in revelation. This has the advantage of focusing attention on the immediate and continuing relevance of the biblical faith as constant effort is made to help a person find the meaning of what is happening in his own life within the context of his relationship with God. Moreover, the belief that the essence of truth contained within traditional Christian concepts can be communicated and appropriated subjectively through one's relationships fosters that very sensitivity to other persons which is often overshadowed by other concerns in the first general approach to the Bible.

On the other hand, there are undesirable results here, too. It is agreed that analysis of what is happening to oneself and of the nature of one's relationships with others is therapeutic and even essential to change, when such analysis takes place in moderation. Too frequent reflection upon one's experiences tends to self-centeredness, to making one's feelings the point of authoritative reference. "People ask how they should feel instead of what they should trust, believe, and serve."[3] Eventually this procedure becomes deleterious to one's spiritual life. As Kierkegaard says, "It is well enough known to physiologists that nothing is more injurious to digestion than constant reflection upon digestion."[4] Furthermore, it is possible to detect in this approach the unintended but implicit assumption that Christian fellowship redeems, whereas surely it is always and only God who redeems.

There may be unresolvable dilemmas proposed here. Or the awareness of the dilemmas may enable one to hold together in proper tension and balance the objective and subjective factors in the biblical revelation and in one's understanding of how that revelation may be appropriated.

Belief and Action

What is intended here is only to raise a question which arises from the educators' wholesale rejection of the moralistic concentration on conduct and "application" of the Bible in earlier religious education, a question which could be answered only with considerable further investigation and thought. The current tendency is to say that a person's actions are the expression of what he believes and is by virtue of his relationship to God. Christian education is constrained today to interpret and amplify this statement, which is not to be disputed. But does the statement offer adequate guidance for the teacher on how he may help his pupils know what form their conduct as Christians may most appropriately assume? What help can be given to a person as he responds to God through the demands of the moment?

Earlier in this century a keen concern with the ethical life, combined with an attitude toward the Bible which forced its use whether or not it was applicable, resulted in a superficial consideration of conduct and a moralistic use of the Bible that are rightly to be rejected. But the vociferous concern which has made a shibboleth of the term "moralism" seems also to have blocked the way for an adequate dealing with the form of the ethical life. Is there any validity in the premise that just as belief affects action, so action affects belief, and that there is need for direct consideration of the two, separately as well as in conjunction with one another?

Or again, it is said that law and gospel always come together—sometimes that the law is the form of the gospel. Is it not therefore a contradiction in terms to refuse to consider the law directly, or to neglect the relationship which may exist between the law and the appropriation of the gospel? With reference to his third use of the moral law, Calvin states that although believers are so "influenced and actuated by the Spirit . . . that they desire to obey God," it is nevertheless true that they profit from exhortation about and meditation upon the law. "For it is the best instrument for enabling them daily to learn with greater truth and certainty what that will of the Lord is which they aspire to follow, and to confirm them in this knowledge."[5] Men need also, and primarily, in Calvin's terms, the study of the Christian doctrine which transforms them into itself, but not in isolation from a consideration of the law and of the obligations of covenant life lived in the world.

Many scholars write directly and helpfully of various aspects of ethical living as it springs from commitment to the living God. Karl Barth speaks of the relationship between the "being" and the "doing" of a person. Randolph Crump Miller points out that from birth to death human beings need "a structure of law and order," and that it is the responsibility of Christian education to provide an understanding of that structure. C. T. Craig, in his description of the two uses of the Bible, indicates that it is quite appropriate for persons to deal directly with the "works" aspect of Christianity, carrying out deliberations against a background of direct consideration of the "gospel." Ramifications of the subject of ethics are endless, leading beyond individual decision and conduct to the whole field of social and political action, and other writers than the ones mentioned have made valuable contributions to various aspects of the subject.

On the other hand, the impression remains that church school teachers need more practical help in knowing what they are to substitute for the "moralistic" teaching they rightly join with philosophers of Christian education in condemning. They are led to speak to pupils frequently of the "eyes of faith" without knowing how to relate this perspective to the volitional factor in education, or to the essential relationship between law and gospel. And surely it is the case that one's response to God cannot be expressed in a vacuum; moral effort seems to be necessary to a person if he is to know the meaning and the reality of his relationship with God. A person seems to need the aid of the church in knowing the direction in which he must move in actualizing the new life which is his, and which is being brought into existence through his struggle.

Ultimately, of course, the answer lies nowhere else than in developing that kind of understanding of the Christian life which views it as a life of obedient response from new beings in Jesus Christ. That is the premise which has been made by all the writers studied. Perhaps, in addition, some help will come through being freed from that kind of irrational reverence for the Bible which compels persons to prooftext every consideration of ethical decision with a particular passage. That kind of view of the Bible which permits persons to face decisions as Christians, changed themselves as persons and guided by the total perspective of the biblical message, will eventually help solve the problem of moralism. And a part of the answer lies in the direction of a methodology which will make it possible for persons to witness to one another about their understanding of the meaning of the biblical revelation for particular situations—not legalistically or in judgment, but as neighbors and friends to one another, bound together within the *koinonia*.

Analysis and Synthesis

With the current emphasis on the unity, the message, the drama of the Bible, it is self-evident that synthesis rather than analysis is the order of the day. This is almost an exact reversal of earlier tendencies to analyze, even to dissect the Bible, with a resultant fragmentation which was indeed deplorable.

But is the pendulum now swinging too far in the other direction? Educationally, it is known that generalizations are meaningful only in terms of the particulars to which they have reference, and which are, in fact, the essential content serving as a basis for the interpretation set forth in the generalizations. Therefore, there must be a constant movement between the general and the particular, the interpretation and the basis or illustration of the interpretation. Likewise, the educator knows that the person who speaks in terms of generalities, interpretations, trends, without being able to document his statements with a wealth of details, often has no real knowledge, and often becomes only a reflection of the emptiness he verbalizes.

The point here is that the current approach to the Bible is a needed complement to the contributions of the previous generation, but that if Christian education is to be effective it must hold together in proper perspective the movement from analysis to synthesis and back again to analysis. This is of special significance for a regular, systematic Bible study which today seems somewhat overbalanced in the direction of synthesis.

Form and Content

Almost all that has been said in this section of the summary relates directly or indirectly to communication and appropriation of the biblical message, for that is the area of special concern of Christian education. And what is suggested now, in a quite tentative way, is that the role of Christian education in relationship to the biblical witness to revelation, to creed or doctrine, is somewhat analogous to the relationship between form and content, between the institutional church and the life which is its inner spirit, between the "becoming" and the "being" of a person. Christian education is still seeking to find its role in the Christian community, and the question here becomes one concerning the role of Christian education in the communication of the biblical faith, rather than concerning the role of the Bible in Christian education.

Traditionally, Christian education has often been assumed to be means to an end; methods have been selected as being suitable devices by which one might arrive at predetermined goals or by which one might communicate certain content. Organization has been viewed as a vehicle quite external to the reality with which it was concerned. There is a truth in these views, because certainly the educational process and structure must be considered independently from the vantage point of technical reason, and they may be distinguished from the content with which they deal; and certainly Christian education is a relative form and has no life or purpose of its own.

But there is also an inadequacy in views which speak of methods, organization, Christian education, always in terms of means and ends. The terminology makes the structure, the dynamic movement, seem to be quite extraneous to the content with which it deals. Such a separation is comparable to what Tillich deplores as the separation of technical and ontological reason, and to what A. E. Taylor has in mind when he says, "The hard and fast distinction between end and means, effect and instrument, a distinction in fact borrowed from the realm of industry, if taken over-seriously, is as pernicious in the theory of art as it is in the theory of morals."[6] Kierkegaard holds that "the profound and elegant thing in relation to spirit is the fact that the *mode of acquisition* and *the possession* are one," and that "in the spiritual world the form is the reduplication of the content."[7]

No terminology is finally satisfactory in its description of the relationship of Christian education to the biblical witness. Form and content may suggest, falsely, that form is identical with content, or that form is determined solely by content, or that Christian education is made sacrosanct by virtue of its relationship to content. All that is intended here is to venture the belief that because the purpose of Christian education inheres within the content with which it is concerned, Christian education as structure and process must be understood, at least in part, as expression of that content. But also, insights from many disciplines of thought are valid when they are considered in relationship to the biblical message, and thereby become the habits, structures, practices, transformed by that message into the forms through which it is communicated. Yet those forms are never unfailingly infallible channels of communication, and Christian education knows itself to be the servant and not the master of revelation.

Acknowledgments

Chapter I. A CHANGING PERSPECTIVE FOR CHRISTIAN EDUCATION

1. Harry Emerson Fosdick, *The Modern Use of the Bible* (New York: The Macmillan Company, 1924), p. 6.
2. There are many excellent comprehensive treatments of the subject. See especially John Dillenberger and Claude Welch, *Protestant Christianity Interpreted Through Its Development* (New York: Charles Scribner's Sons, 1954). Chapters IX and X are particularly pertinent.
3. George Albert Coe, *A Social Theory of Religious Education* (New York: Charles Scribner's Sons, 1917), p. 55.
4. It is interesting to note that a student of Coe's quotes him as saying he arrived independently at the same conclusions as Dewey with respect to democracy in education, the social emphasis, the concept of education as life, and the reconstruction of experience. See article by George P. Michaelides, "A One Time Secretary Writes," *Religious Education* XLVII (March-April, 1952), p. 101.
5. George Albert Coe, *What Is Christian Education?* (New York: Charles Scribner's Sons, 1930), p. 29.
6. *A Social Theory of Religious Education,* p. 102.
7. *Ibid.,* p. 113.
8. William Clayton Bower, *The Curriculum of Religious Education* (New York: Charles Scribner's Sons, 1925), p. 128.
9. *Ibid.,* p. 35.
10. *Ibid.,* p. vii.
11. *Ibid.,* p. 206.
12. William Clayton Bower, *The Living Bible* (New York: Harper & Brothers, 1936), p. 12. Used by permission.
13. See, for example, Harold Hunting, *The Story of Our Bible: How It Grew to Be What It Is* (New York: Charles Scribner's Sons, 1915); George Hodges, *How to Know the Bible* (Indianapolis: Bobbs-Merrill Company, 1918); Muriel Streibert, *Youth and the Bible* (New York: The Macmillan Company, 1924); Edna Baxter, *How Our Religion Began* (New York: Harper & Brothers, 1939); T. G. Soares, *The Origins of the Bible* (New York: Harper & Brothers, 1941).
14. Ethel Smither, *The Use of the Bible with Children* (Nashville: Abingdon Press, 1937), p. 22. Used by permission.
15. Paul H. Vieth, *How to Teach in the Church School* (Philadelphia: The Westminster Press, 1935), p. 48.
16. Adelaide Case, *Liberal Christianity and Religious Education* (New York: The Macmillan Company, 1924). See especially p. 99.
17. Walter Athearn, *The Minister and the Teacher* (New York: The Century Company, 1932), pp. 162-165 *et passim.*
18. For one example, see Luther Allan Weigle, *Jesus and the Educational Method* (New York: Abingdon Press, 1939).

19. Paul H. Vieth, *Objectives in Religious Education* (New York: Harper & Brothers, 1930) , p. 88.

20. *Ibid.*

21. Erwin Shaver, *Present-Day Trends in Religious Education* (Boston: Pilgrim Press, 1929) , pp. 94 ff.

22. Georgia Harkness, "An Underlying Philosophy for Religious Education," *Studies in Religious Education,* eds. Philip Henry Lotz and L. W. Crawford (Nashville: Cokesbury Press, 1931), p. 58. Used by permission.

23. E. G. Homrighausen, "The Real Problem of Religious Education," *Religious Education* XXXIV (January-March, 1939) , p. 15.

24. Harrison Elliott, *Can Religious Education Be Christian?* (New York: The Macmillan Company, 1940) , p. 93. Used by permission.

25. *Ibid.,* p. 113.

26. H. Shelton Smith, *Faith and Nurture* (New York: Charles Scribner's Sons, 1941) , p. 29.

27. *Ibid.,* p. 110.

28. *Christian Education Today* (Chicago: International Council of Religion, 1940) . See especially pp. 9, 11, 12.

29. See article by J. Howard Howson, "The Harvard, Columbia and Princeton Reports on General Education," *Religious Education* XLII (January-February, 1947) , pp. 76-79. These reports, all of the same general tenor as the outstanding Harvard report, seem to Howson to mark the "end of an era" when "it mattered little what a person studied as long as his interest was captured to the extent of commanding his sustained effort for thorough scholarly study."

30. *General Education in a Free Society* (Cambridge: Harvard University Press, 1945) , p. 176.

31. Cf. *ibid.,* pp. 47-50.

32. *Ibid.,* p. 78.

33. *Ibid.,* p. 105.

34. Paul H. Vieth, *The Church and Christian Education* (St. Louis: Bethany Press, 1947) , p. 62.

35. *Ibid.*

36. *Ibid.,* p. 63.

37. *Ibid.,* p. 80.

38. *Ibid.*

39. Cf. *ibid.,* pp. 74 ff.

40. Quoted in Bernhard W. Anderson, "Changing Emphases in Biblical Scholarship," *Journal of Bible and Religion* XXIII (April, 1955) , p. 82.

41. Lewis J. Sherrill, *The Gift of Power* (New York: The Macmillan Company, 1955) , p. 68. Used by permission.

42. John Baillie, *The Idea of Revelation in Recent Thought* (New York: Columbia University Press, 1956) , pp. 3-4.

Chapter II. THE THEOLOGICAL INFLUENCE

1. Walter M. Horton, "Contemporary Protestant Theology and the Bible," *Journal of Religious Thought* XIII (Autumn-Winter, 1955-56) , pp. 31-42.

2. William Temple, *Nature, Man and God* (London: Macmillan and Company Ltd., 1934) , pp. 499-500.

3. *Ibid.,* pp. 328-355.

4. *Ibid.,* p. 345.

5. *Ibid.,* p. 315.

6. *Ibid.,* p. 499.

7. *Ibid.,* p. 317.

8. *Ibid.*, p. 354.

9. William Temple, *Christ the Truth* (New York: The Macmillan Company, 1924) , p. 184.

10. *Ibid.*, p. 185.

11. Cf. *Nature, Man and God*, p. 5.

12. Cf. *Christ the Truth*, p. 4; *Nature, Man and God*, pp. 474-475.

13. *Nature, Man and God*, p. 261.

14. *Ibid.*, p. 315.

15. *Ibid.*, p. 314.

16. *Ibid.*, p. 263.

17. *Ibid.*, p. 312.

18. *Ibid.*, p. 495.

19. Karl Barth, *Church Dogmatics*, Vol. I, Part I, *The Doctrine of the Word of God*, trans. G. T. Thomson (Edinburgh: T. & T. Clark, 1936, 1955) , p. 133.

20. Claude Welch, *In This Name: The Doctrine of the Trinity in Contemporary Theology* (New York: Charles Scribner's Sons, 1952) , p. 169. Used by permission.

21. Karl Barth, *The Epistle to the Romans*, trans. Edwyn Hoskyns (6th edition; London: Oxford University Press, 1933) , p. 35.

22. *The Doctrine of the Word of God*, Vol. I, Part II, trans. G. T. Thomson and Harold Knight (Edinburgh: T. & T. Clark, 1956) , p. 714.

23. *The Doctrine of the Word of God*, Vol. I, Part I, p. 122.

24. *The Doctrine of the Word of God*, Vol. I, Part II, p. 463.

25. *The Doctrine of the Word of God*, Vol. I, Part I, p. 127.

26. *Ibid.*, p. 149.

27. *The Doctrine of the Word of God*, Vol. I, Part II, p. 464.

28. *Ibid.*, pp. 532-533.

29. Cf. *ibid.*

30. *The Doctrine of the Word of God*, Vol. I, Part I, p. 226.

31. *The Doctrine of the Word of God*, Vol. I, Part II, p. 727.

32. *Ibid.*, p. 736.

33. *Ibid.*, p. 737.

34. *Ibid.*, p. 738.

35. *Ibid.*, p. 454.

36. Paul Tillich, "The World Situation," *The Christian Answer*, ed. Henry Van Dusen (New York: Charles Scribner's Sons, 1945) , p. 31. Used by permission.

37. Paul Tillich, *Systematic Theology*, Vol. I (Chicago: University of Chicago Press, 1951) , p. 3.

38. Cf. *ibid.*, p. 60.

39. *Ibid.*, p. 61.

40. *Ibid.*, p. 64.

41. *Ibid.*, p. 48.

42. *Ibid.*, p. 49.

43. *Ibid.*, p. 74.

44. *Ibid.*, p. 75.

45. *Ibid.*, p. 108.

46. *Ibid.*, p. 110.

47. *Ibid.*, p. 118.

48. *Ibid.*, p. 111.

49. *Ibid.*, p. 126.

50. *Ibid.*

51. Paul Tillich, "Religious Symbols and Our Knowledge of God," *The Christian Scholar* XXXVIII (September, 1955) , p. 192.

52. *Ibid.*, p. 191.
53. *Systematic Theology*, Vol. I, p. 137.
54. *Ibid.*, p. 34.
55. *Ibid.*
56. *Ibid.*, p. 35.
57. *Ibid.*
58. *Ibid.*, p. 159.
59. *Ibid.*
60. *Ibid.*
61. *Ibid.*, p. 35.
62. Paul Tillich, *Biblical Religion and the Search for Ultimate Reality* (Chicago: University of Chicago Press, 1955) , p. 13.
63. From *Revelation and Reason* by Emil Brunner, trans. Olive Wyon, p. 8. Copyright 1946, by W. L. Jenkins, The Westminster Press. Used by permission.
64. Emil Brunner, *Dogmatics*, Vol. II, *The Christian Doctrine of Creation and Redemption*, trans. Olive Wyon (London: Lutterworth Press, 1952) , p. v.
65. *Ibid.*, p. vi.
66. Emil Brunner, *Dogmatics*, Vol. I, *The Christian Doctrine of God*, trans. Olive Wyon (London: Lutterworth Press, 1949) , p. 15.
67. *Ibid.*, p. 16.
68. *Ibid.*, p. 17.
69. *Ibid.*, p. 20.
70. *Ibid.*
71. Emil Brunner, *The Divine-Human Encounter*, trans. Amandus W. Loos (Philadelphia: The Westminster Press, 1943), p. 74. Used by permission.
72. *The Christian Doctrine of God*, p. 20.
73. *The Christian Doctrine of Creation and Redemption*, p. 257.
74. *Ibid.*, p. 215. See especially note 2.
75. *Ibid.*, p. 216.
76. *The Christian Doctrine of God*, p. 110.
77. Cf. *ibid.*, pp. 132-136. Brunner points out that he had unfortunately helped foster the mistaken idea that the two terms were to be equated.
78. *The Christian Doctrine of Creation and Redemption*, p. 26.
79. *The Christian Doctrine of God*, p. 19.
80. H. Richard Niebuhr, *The Meaning of Revelation* (New York: The Macmillan Company, 1946) , p. 41.
81. *Ibid.*, p. 109.
82. *Ibid.*, p. 43.
83. *Ibid.*, p. 89.
84. *Ibid.*, p. 58.
85. *Ibid.*, p. 72.
86. *Ibid.*
87. *Ibid.*, p. 73.
88. *Ibid.*, p. 93.
89. *Ibid.*, p. 152.
90. *Ibid.*
91. *Ibid.*, p. 154.
92. *Ibid.*, p. 46.
93. *Ibid.*, p. 127.
94. *Ibid.*, p. 89.
95. *Ibid.*, pp. 175-176.
96. *Ibid.*, p. 182.
97. *Ibid.*, p. 131.
98. *Ibid.*
99. *Ibid.*, p. 162.

100. *Ibid.*, p. 165.
101. *Ibid.*, pp. 166-167.
102. *Ibid.*, p. 168.
103. Bernhard Anderson, *Rediscovering the Bible* (New York: Association Press, 1951) . See G. Ernest Wright, "The Study of the Old Testament," *Protestant Thought in the Twentieth Century*, ed. Arnold Nash (New York: The Macmillan Company, 1951) , p. 43, footnote.
104. Cf. Amos Wilder, "New Testament Theology in Transition," *The Study of the Bible Today and Tomorrow*, ed. Harold R. Willoughby (Chicago: University of Chicago Press, 1947) , p. 420.
105. Cf. James Smart, "The Death and Rebirth of Old Testament Theology," *The Journal of Religion* XXIII (1943) , pp. 1-11, 125-136.
106. Cf. Clarence T. Craig, "Biblical Theology and the Rise of Historicism," *Journal of Biblical Literature* LXII (1943) , p. 294.
107. H. H. Rowley, *The Relevance of the Bible* (New York: The Macmillan Company, 1944) , p. 13.
108. Paul Tillich, *Systematic Theology*, Vol. II (Chicago: University of Chicago Press, 1957) , p. 107.
109. Cf. James Muilenburg, "The Return to Old Testament Theology," *Christianity and the Contemporary Scene*, eds. Randolph C. Miller and Henry H. Shires (New York: Morehouse-Gorham Company, 1943) , pp. 31-32.
110. "Guiding Principles for the Interpretation of the Bible," *Biblical Authority for Today*, eds. Alan Richardson and Wolfgang Schweitzer (London: SCM Press Ltd., 1951) , pp. 240-241.
111. Floyd Filson, "The Study of the New Testament," *Protestant Thought in the Twentieth Century*, p. 64.
112. Emil G. Kraeling, *The Old Testament Since the Reformation* (New York: Harper & Brothers, 1955), p. 271. Used by permission.
113. Schweitzer, "Biblical Theology and Ethics Today," *Biblical Authority for Today*, p. 130.
114. Wright, *op. cit.*, p. 39.
115. *The Study of the Bible Today and Tomorrow*, p. xv.
116. Comments on James R. Branton, "Our Present Situation in Biblical Theology," *Religion in Life* XXVI (Winter, 1956-57) , p. 30.
117. Filson, *op. cit.*, p. 67.
118. Hubert Cunliffe-Jones, *The Authority of the Biblical Revelation* (London: James Clarke & Company, 1945) , p. 10.

Chapter III. THE MEANING OF REVELATION

1. James D. Smart, *The Teaching Ministry of the Church* (Philadelphia: The Westminster Press, 1954). Quoted material used by permission.
2. *Ibid.*, p. 89.
3. *Ibid.*
4. *Ibid.*
5. *Ibid.*, p. 90.
6. *Ibid.*
7. *Ibid.*, p. 91.
8. Cf. James D. Smart, *What a Man Can Believe* (Philadelphia: The Westminster Press, 1943) , pp. 76-80. Quotations from this volume are used by permission of the publishers.
9. *Ibid.*, p. 47.
10. *Ibid.*, p. 51.
11. *Ibid.*, p. 7.
12. *The Teaching Ministry of the Church*, p. 33.

13. *Ibid.*, p. 24.
14. *Ibid.*
15. *Ibid.*, p. 45.
16. *Ibid.*, p. 41.
17. *What a Man Can Believe*, p. 82.
18. *The Teaching Ministry of the Church*, p. 159.
19. *Ibid.*, p. 19.
20. *Ibid.*
21. *Ibid.*
22. *Ibid.*, p. 20.
23. *Ibid.*
24. *Ibid.*, p. 19.
25. *Ibid.*, p. 25.
26. *Ibid.*
27. *Ibid.*, p. 125.
28. *Ibid.*, p. 37.
29. *Ibid.*, p. 90.
30. *Ibid.*, p. 36.
31. *Ibid.*, p. 122.
32. *Ibid.*, p. 129 *et passim*.
33. *Ibid.*, p. 107.
34. *Ibid.*
35. Randolph Crump Miller, *The Clue to Christian Education* (New York: Charles Scribner's Sons, 1950) , p. 74. Used by permission.
36. *Ibid.*, p. 5.
37. *Ibid.*, p. 4.
38. From the book, *Education for Christian Living*, by Randolph Crump Miller, p. 9. © 1956 by Prentice-Hall, Inc., Englewood Cliffs, N. J. Used by permission.
39. *Ibid.*, p. 12.
40. *The Clue to Christian Education*, p. 17.
41. *Education for Christian Living*, p. 12.
42. *The Clue to Christian Education*, p. 37.
43. Randolph Crump Miller, *Biblical Theology and Christian Education* (New York: Charles Scribner's Sons, 1956) , p. 37. Used by permission.
44. *The Clue to Christian Education*, pp. 37-38.
45. *Ibid.*, p. 38.
46. *Biblical Theology and Christian Education*, p. 198.
47. Randolph Crump Miller, *Religion Makes Sense* (New York: Wilcox & Follett, 1950) , p. 262.
48. *Ibid.*, pp. 262-263, footnote.
49. "Empirical Method and Its Critics," *Anglican Theological Review* XXVII (reprint; January, 1945) , p. 31.
50. Randolph Crump Miller, *What We Can Believe* (New York: Charles Scribner's Sons, 1941), pp. 202, 209. Used by permission.
51. *Ibid.*, p. 219.
52. "Empirical Method and Its Critics," p. 32.
53. *The Clue to Christian Education*, p. 43.
54. *Education for Christian Living*, p. 12. Italics mine.
55. *Religion Makes Sense*, p. 296.
56. *The Clue to Christian Education*, p. vii.
57. *Religion Makes Sense*, p. 260.
58. *What We Can Believe*, p. 56.
59. *The Clue to Christian Education*, p. 38.
60. *Education for Christian Living*, p. 89.

61. *Ibid.*
62. *Ibid.*, p. 66.
63. *Biblical Theology and Christian Education*, p. 13.
64. *The Clue to Christian Education*, p. 88.
65. *Ibid.*
66. *Ibid.*
67. Randolph Crump Miller, *Guide for Church School Teachers* (Greenwich, Connecticut: Seabury Press, 1943). See especially p. 79.
68. *Christianity and the Contemporary Scene*, eds. Randolph Crump Miller and Henry H. Shires (New York: Morehouse-Gorham Company, 1943), pp. 196-200.
69. *The Clue to Christian Education*, p. 15.
70. *Ibid.*, pp. 18-19.
71. *Ibid.*, p. 6.
72. Randolph Crump Miller, "Education Is for Redemption," *World Christian Education* X (Fourth Quarter, 1955), p. 112. See also "Education for Redemption," *A Symphony of the Christian Year* (Greenwich, Connecticut: Seabury Press, 1954), pp. 12-18.
73. *The Clue to Christian Education*, p. 8.
74. *Education for Christian Living*, p. 12.
75. *Ibid.*, p. 67.
76. Lewis J. Sherrill, *The Gift of Power* (New York: The Macmillan Company, 1955), p. 65. Used by permission.
77. *Ibid.*
78. *Ibid.*, p. xii.
79. *Ibid.*, pp. 68-69.
80. *Ibid.*, p. 69.
81. *Ibid.*
82. *Ibid.*, p. 110.
83. *Ibid.*, p. 78.
84. *Ibid.*, p. 86.
85. *Ibid.*, p. 77.
86. *Ibid.*, p. 87.
87. *Ibid.*, pp. 93-94.
88. Lewis J. Sherrill, "Basic Considerations," Part III: Revelation and Education (mimeographed syllabus for Religious Education Course 103, The Educational Ministry of the Church, Union Theological Seminary, New York), p. 3.
89. *The Gift of Power*, p. 70.
90. *Ibid.*, p. 73.
91. *Ibid.*, p. 74.
92. *Ibid.*
93. *Ibid.*
94. *Ibid.*, p. 76.
95. *Ibid.*, p. 77.
96. "Basic Considerations," p. 3.
97. *The Gift of Power*, p. 78.
98. *Ibid.*
99. Lewis J. Sherrill, *The Rise of Christian Education* (New York: The Macmillan Company, 1944), pp. 98-99. Used by permission.
100. Lewis J. Sherrill, *Guilt and Redemption* (revised edition; Richmond: John Knox Press, 1957), pp. 215-216.
101. *The Rise of Christian Education*, p. 300.
102. "Basic Considerations," p. 1.
103. *The Gift of Power*, p. xi.

104. *Ibid.*, p. 82.
105. *Ibid.*, p. 88.
106. *Ibid.*, p. 83.
107. *Ibid.*
108. *Ibid.*, pp. 90-91.
109. D. Campbell Wyckoff, *The Gospel and Christian Education* (Philadelphia: The Westminster Press, 1959), p. 92. Used by permission.
110. Iris V. Cully, *The Dynamics of Christian Education* (Philadelphia: The Westminster Press, 1958).
111. Paul H. Vieth, "The Content of the Curriculum," *Religious Education* XLVII (September-October, 1952), p. 310.
112. Paul H. Vieth, *The Church School: The Organization, Administration, and Supervision of Christian Education in the Local Church* (Philadelphia: Christian Education Press, 1957), p. 17 *et passim*.

Chapter IV. THE NATURE OF THE BIBLICAL WITNESS

1. James D. Smart, *What a Man Can Believe*, p. 76.
2. *Ibid.*, p. 58.
3. *Ibid.*, p. 76.
4. *Ibid.*, p. 75.
5. *Ibid.*, pp. 80-81.
6. James D. Smart, *The Teaching Ministry of the Church*, p. 25.
7. *Ibid.*, p. 118.
8. *What a Man Can Believe*, p. 66.
9. *The Teaching Ministry of the Church*, p. 117.
10. *Ibid.*, p. 143.
11. *What a Man Can Believe*, p. 56.
12. *Ibid.*, pp. 56-57.
13. *Ibid.*, p. 65.
14. *Ibid.*
15. *The Teaching Ministry of the Church*, p. 25.
16. *Ibid.*, p. 117.
17. *Ibid.*, p. 36.
18. *What a Man Can Believe*, p. 77.
19. David Noel Freedman and James D. Smart, *God Has Spoken* (Philadelphia: The Westminster Press, 1949), p. 30. Used by permission.
20. *The Teaching Ministry of the Church*, p. 140.
21. *Ibid.*, p. 143.
22. *Ibid.*, p. 142.
23. *Ibid.*, p. 144.
24. *Ibid.*
25. *Ibid.*, p. 116.
26. *Ibid.*, p. 152.
27. *Ibid.*, p. 118.
28. *Ibid.*, p. 119.
29. Randolph Crump Miller, *Biblical Theology and Christian Education*, p. 167.
30. *Ibid.*
31. Randolph Crump Miller, *The Clue to Christian Education*, p. 16.
32. Randolph Crump Miller, *Education for Christian Living*, p. 49.
33. *Biblical Theology and Christian Education*, p. 20.
34. *Education for Christian Living*, p. 49.
35. *Biblical Theology and Christian Education*, p. vii.
36. *Ibid.*, pp. 16-17.

37. *Ibid.*
38. *The Clue to Christian Education,* p. 170.
39. Randolph Crump Miller, "Authority and Freedom in Doctrine," *Episco-palians United,* ed. Theodore Ferris (New York: Morehouse-Gorham Company, 1948) , p. 21.
40. *Ibid.,* p. 20.
41. *Ibid.*
42. *The Clue to Christian Education,* p. 170.
43. *Ibid.,* p. 174.
44. "Authority and Freedom in Doctrine," p. 34.
45. *The Clue to Christian Education,* p. 171.
46. *Ibid.,* p. 172.
47. "Authority and Freedom in Doctrine," pp. 24-25.
48. *The Clue to Christian Education,* p. 173.
49. "Authority and Freedom in Doctrine," p. 23.
50. *Ibid.,* p. 28.
51. *Biblical Theology and Christian Education,* p. 211.
52. *The Clue to Christian Education,* p. 176.
53. "Authority and Freedom in Doctrine," p. 22.
54. *Biblical Theology and Christian Education,* p. 203.
55. *Ibid.*
56. *Ibid.,* p. 195.
57. *Ibid.,* p. 196.
58. *Ibid.,* p. 204.
59. *Ibid.,* p. 29.
60. *Ibid.*
61. Lewis J. Sherrill, *The Gift of Power,* p. 13.
62. *Ibid.*
63. *Ibid.,* p. 117.
64. Lewis J. Sherrill, *Guilt and Redemption,* p. 170.
65. *Ibid.,* p. 171.
66. *Ibid.*
67. Lewis J. Sherrill, *The Rise of Christian Education,* pp. 93-94.
68. *Guilt and Redemption,* p. 173.
69. *The Rise of Christian Education,* p. 109.
70. *Guilt and Redemption,* p. 173.
71. Lewis J. Sherrill, *The Struggle of the Soul* (New York: The Macmillan Company, 1951), p. 66. Used by permission.
72. *Ibid.*
73. *The Rise of Christian Education,* p. 96.
74. *The Struggle of the Soul,* p. 68.
75. *Ibid.,* p. 66.
76. *The Gift of Power,* p. 110.
77. *Ibid.,* p. 109.
78. *Ibid.,* p. 110.
79. *Ibid.*
80. *Ibid.,* pp. 110-111.
81. *Ibid.,* p. 111.
82. *Ibid.*
83. *Ibid.,* p. 99.
84. *Ibid.,* p. 95.
85. *Ibid.,* p. 96.
86. *Ibid.,* p. 98.
87. *Ibid.*
88. *The Struggle of the Soul,* p. 69.

89. *Ibid.*, p. 68.
90. *Ibid.*, p. 67.
91. *Ibid.*, p. 98.
92. *Ibid.*, p. 99.
93. *The Gift of Power*, p. 100.
94. *Ibid.*
95. *Ibid.*, p. 101.
96. Howard Grimes, "Christianity Is Learned Through Living Encounter with the Bible," *The Minister and Christian Nurture*, ed. Nathaniel F. Forsyth (New York: Abingdon Press, 1957).
97. Allen O. Miller, *Invitation to Theology: Resources for Christian Nurture and Discipline* (Philadelphia: Christian Education Press, 1958).

Chapter V. THE RELEVANCE OF THE BIBLE

1. Bernhard Anderson, *Rediscovering the Bible* (New York: Association Press, 1951), p. 22.
2. James D. Smart, *The Teaching Ministry of the Church*, p. 157.
3. *Ibid.*, p. 146.
4. *Ibid.*, p. 77.
5. *Ibid.*, p. 22.
6. *Ibid.*, p. 21.
7. *Ibid.*
8. *Ibid.*, p. 22.
9. *Ibid.*, p. 23.
10. *Ibid.*, p. 157.
11. *Ibid.*, p. 155.
12. *Ibid.*, p. 157.
13. *Ibid.*, p. 158.
14. *Ibid.*
15. David Noel Freedman and James D. Smart, *God Has Spoken*, p. 12.
16. *The Teaching Ministry of the Church*, p. 157.
17. *Ibid.*, p. 43.
18. *God Has Spoken*, p. 45.
19. Cf. *The Teaching Ministry of the Church*, pp. 118, 151-152.
20. Randolph Crump Miller, *Biblical Theology and Christian Education*, p. 16.
21. *Ibid.*, p. 17.
22. Randolph Crump Miller, *The Clue to Christian Education*, p. 4.
23. *Biblical Theology and Christian Education*, p. 5.
24. Randolph Crump Miller, *Education for Christian Living*, p. 7.
25. *Biblical Theology and Christian Education*, p. vii.
26. *Ibid.*, p. 4.
27. *Ibid.*, p. 2.
28. *Ibid.*, p. 29.
29. *Education for Christian Living*, p. 65.
30. *Ibid.* See *Biblical Theology and Christian Education*, pp. 16-66, for fuller statement.
31. *Education for Christian Living*, p. 65.
32. *Ibid.*
33. *Ibid.*
34. *Ibid.*, p. 369.
35. *Biblical Theology and Christian Education*, p. 170.
36. *Ibid.*, pp. 170-171.
37. *Ibid.*, p. 171.

38. *The Clue to Christian Education*, p. 5.
39. *Ibid.*, p. 14.
40. Lewis J. Sherrill, *The Gift of Power*, p. 105.
41. *Ibid.*
42. *Ibid.*, p. 198, note 1, Ch. V.
43. *Ibid.*, p. 105.
44. *Ibid.*, p. 117.
45. *Ibid.*, pp. 93-94.
46. *Ibid.*, p. 176.
47. *Ibid.*, p. 175.
48. "Basic Considerations," p. 6.
49. *The Gift of Power*, p. 175.
50. *Ibid.*, p. 107.
51. *Ibid.*, p. 181.
52. *Ibid.*, pp. 107-108.
53. "Basic Considerations," p. 6.
54. *The Gift of Power*, p. 41.
55. *Ibid.*, p. 43.
56. *Ibid.*, p. 97.
57. *Ibid.*
58. *Ibid.*
59. *Ibid.*, p. 59.
60. *Ibid.*, p. 182.
61. *Ibid.*, p. 104.
62. *Ibid.*, p. 116.
63. *Ibid.*
64. Lewis J. Sherrill, *The Rise of Christian Education*, p. 82.
65. *Ibid.*, pp. 87-88.
66. *Ibid.*, p. 83.
67. *Ibid.*, p. 88.
68. Lewis J. Sherrill, "Theme and Predicament" (mimeographed statement used with Religious Education Course 230, The Bible in Religious Education, Union Theological Seminary, New York) , Part VIII.
69. Lewis J. Sherrill, *Guilt and Redemption*, p. 232.
70. *Ibid.*, p. 218.
71. *The Gift of Power*, p. 116.
72. *The Rise of Christian Education*, p. 134.
73. Paul H. Vieth, "The Content of the Curriculum," *Religious Education* XLVII (September-October, 1952) , p. 311.
74. *Ibid.*
75. Reuel L. Howe, *Man's Need and God's Action* (Greenwich, Connecticut: The Seabury Press, Inc., 1953) . See Sherrill's comment in *The Gift of Power*, p. 196, note 1, Chapter III.
76. Clarence Tucker Craig, *The Use of the Bible in Teaching* (Reprint from *The Church School;* Nashville: The Editorial Division, Board of Education of the Methodist Church, 1942) , p. 6.
77. *Ibid.*, p. 8.

Chapter VI. THE APPROPRIATION OF THE BIBLICAL MESSAGE

1. James D. Smart, *The Teaching Ministry of the Church*, p. 25.
2. *Ibid.*, p. 11.
3. James D. Smart, *What a Man Can Believe*, pp. 63-64.
4. *Ibid.*, pp. 65-66.
5. David Noel Freedman and James D. Smart, *God Has Spoken*, p. 27.

6. *What a Man Can Believe,* p. 23.
7. *Ibid.,* p. 79.
8. *The Teaching Ministry of the Church,* p. 167.
9. *Ibid.*
10. *Ibid.*
11. *Ibid.,* p. 61.
12. *Ibid.,* p. 66.
13. *Ibid.,* pp. 144-153.
14. *Ibid.,* pp. 147-148.
15. *Ibid.,* p. 149.
16. *Ibid.,* p. 152.
17. *Ibid.,* p. 116. Smart is again drawing upon what is already being done. Elsewhere, he points to church picnics and Christmas pageants as means of building fellowship across age group lines (p. 124). Is he or is he not saying that a new approach must be devised to fit the new theology?
18. *Ibid.,* p. 119.
19. *Ibid.,* p. 168.
20. *Ibid.,* p. 169.
21. *Ibid.*
22. *Ibid.,* p. 183.
23. *Ibid.,* p. 113.
24. *Ibid.,* pp. 116-130.
25. *Ibid.,* p. 111.
26. *Ibid.,* p. 162.
27. *Ibid.,* p. 165.
28. *Ibid.*
29. *Ibid.,* p. 166.
30. *Ibid.*
31. *Ibid.,* p. 168.
32. *Ibid.,* p. 169.
33. *Ibid.,* p. 168.
34. *Ibid.*
35. Randolph Crump Miller, "Our Faith and How We Communicate It" (Address given to Teachers of the Weekday Schools of Religion, January 30, 1956. Mimeographed copy available Council of Churches of Syracuse and Onondaga County) , p. 1.
36. Randolph Crump Miller, *Biblical Theology and Christian Education,* p. 33.
37. "Our Faith and How We Communicate It," p. 1.
38. Randolph Crump Miller, *The Clue to Christian Education,* p. 80.
39. *Ibid.,* p. 71.
40. Randolph Crump Miller, *Education for Christian Living,* p. 166.
41. *Ibid.,* pp. 8, 66.
42. *Ibid.,* p. 169.
43. *Ibid.,* p. 171.
44. *The Clue to Christian Education,* p. 4.
45. *Ibid.*
46. *Ibid.,* p. 35.
47. *Education for Christian Living,* p. 166.
48. *Ibid.,* p. 43.
49. Randolph Crump Miller, "Christian Education as a Theological Discipline and Method," *Religious Education* XLVIII (November-December, 1953), p. 412.
50. *The Clue to Christian Education,* p. 4.
51. *Education for Christian Living,* pp. 4, 221-226.

52. *The Clue to Christian Education*, p. 3.
53. *Ibid.*, p. 4.
54. *Education for Christian Living*, p. 143.
55. *Ibid.*, p. 169.
56. *Ibid.*, p. 74.
57. *The Clue to Christian Education*, p. 46.
58. See Randolph Crump Miller's book of sermons, *A Symphony of the Christian Year* (Greenwich, Connecticut: Seabury Press, 1954) , p. v.
59. *Education for Christian Living*, p. 139.
60. *Biblical Theology and Christian Education*, pp. 7 ff.
61. *Ibid.*, p. 113.
62. *Ibid.*, p. 117.
63. *Ibid.*, pp. 118, 128.
64. *Ibid.*, p. 118.
65. *Education for Christian Living*, p. 371.
66. Lewis J. Sherrill, *The Gift of Power*, pp. 45-46.
67. *Ibid.*, p. 89.
68. *Ibid.*, p. 88.
69. *Ibid.*, p. 85.
70. Lewis J. Sherrill, *The Struggle of the Soul*, pp. 12-13.
71. *The Gift of Power*, p. 89.
72. *Ibid.*, p. 99.
73. *Ibid.*, p. 110.
74. *Ibid.*, pp. 98-99.
75. *Ibid.*, pp. 124-126.
76. *Ibid.*, p. 179.
77. Lewis J. Sherrill, *The Rise of Christian Education*, pp. 6-7.
78. *The Gift of Power*, p. 174.
79. *Ibid.*, p. 176.
80. *Ibid.*
81. *Ibid.*, p. 95.
82. *Ibid.*, pp. 183-184.
83. *Ibid.*, pp. 182-183.
84. *Ibid.*, p. 178.
85. *Ibid.*, p. 85.
86. *Ibid.*, p. 120.
87. *Ibid.*, p. 121.
88. *Ibid.*, pp. 184-185.
89. *Ibid.*, p. 187.
90. *Ibid.*, p. 189.
91. *Ibid.*, p. 86.
92. *Ibid.*, p. 191.
93. *Ibid.*, p. 174.
94. *The Rise of Christian Education*, p. 49.
95. *Ibid.*, p. 51.
96. *Ibid.*, p. 98.
97. *The Gift of Power*, p. 155.
98. *Ibid.*, pp. 155-156.
99. *Ibid.*, p. 157.
100. *The Struggle of the Soul*, p. 65.
101. *The Gift of Power*, p. 161.
102. *The Struggle of the Soul*, pp. 21-22.
103. *Ibid.*, p. 124.
104. Iris V. Cully, *The Dynamics of Christian Education*, p. 87.

105. For a statement of presuppositions set forth by this committee as underlying the educational work of the church, see *Christian Education Within the Covenant Community—the Church* (Richmond: Board of Christian Education, Presbyterian Church, U. S., 1958).

Chapter VIII. TOWARD A POINT OF VIEW

1. Søren Kierkegaard, *On Authority and Revelation*, trans. Walter Lowrie (Princeton: Princeton University Press, 1955), p. 165.
2. Karl Barth, *The Doctrine of the Word of God*, Vol. I, Part I, p. 185.
3. P. T. Forsyth, *The Principle of Authority* (London: Hodder and Stoughton, 1908), p. 391.
4. Kierkegaard, *op. cit.*, p. 29.
5. John Calvin, *Institutes of the Christian Religion*, trans. Henry Beveridge (2 vols.; London: James Clarke & Company, 1949), Bk. II, chap. vii, par. 12.
6. A. E. Taylor, *The Faith of a Moralist* (London: Macmillan and Company Ltd., 1930), II, p. 88.
7. Kierkegaard, *op. cit.*, pp. 42, 43.